LET
THE
EARTH
BLESS
THE
LORD

LET THE EARTH BLESS THE LORD

A CHRISTIAN PERSPECTIVE

ON LAND USE

Edited by C.A. Cesaretti
and Stephen Commins

THE SEABURY PRESS   NEW YORK

1981
The Seabury Press
New York, N.Y. 10017

Library of Congress Cataloging in Publication Data

Cesaretti, C   A
Let the Earth bless the Lord.

Bibliography: p.
1. Land use—Biblical teaching—Study and
teaching.   2. Land use—Moral and religious
aspects—Study and teaching.   3. Human ecology—
Moral and religious aspects—Study and teaching.
I. Commins, Stephen, joint author.   II. Title.
BS680.L25C47   241'.64   81-54
ISBN 0-8164-2296-6

Contents

Foreword

In 1979 the 66th General Convention of the Episcopal Church resolved that the National Hunger Committee and its staff:

> develop and communicate such study and action programs as will help members of the Episcopal Church to determine their own position and take informed and appropriate action with respect to agrarian land reforms at home and abroad as these affect world food production.

Let the Earth Bless the Lord had its genesis in this directive of the governing body of the Episcopal Church.

The Rev. Stephen Commins provided many of the rich resources from which this work gains its energy and integrity. His research and incisive approach to a massive bibliography of complex material provided insight and creative focus. Working in close collaboration with Peggy Ducey, Lois McCloskey, and Kathy West, Commins and his resource group prepared the major essays on problems related to land use. Sharon Commins created the cover and interior illustrations for the book.

We are grateful to the National Hunger Committee for their support, especially to Dr. David Crean, Hunger Officer for the Episcopal Church.

To the Presiding Bishop, the Rt. Rev. John M. Allin, and to Alice Emery, Executive for National Mission in Church and Society, we owe a debt of gratitude for their constant encouragement and counsel.

Charles A. Cesaretti
Public Issues Officer
The Episcopal Church

Introduction

In his introduction to Stewart Udall's *The Quiet Crisis,* John F. Kennedy wrote:

> The race between education and erosion, between wisdom and waste has not run its course. . . . The nation's battle to preserve the common estate is far from won. . . . The crisis may be quiet, but it is urgent.

Let the Earth Bless the Lord is about the land, its erosion and waste; it is written out of a genuine sense of urgency. It is also written out of concern and love for the land—a love and concern growing not out of a romantic longing for what-can-be-no-more, but out of a deep theological concern for the *Creation.*

This study guide is not only written out of love for the Creation, it is also written out of love for the *Creator.* It is written in celebration of the Lord's mighty works of creation and redemption. And it is written to glorify God as did the Three Young Men who sang their praises in the fiery furnace with a hymn:

> Let the earth bless the Lord;
> let it sing praises to him and
> highly exalt him for ever. .

This study guide is also written with reverence for the land seen as a grand book spreading its pages before us to be read. It is a testament to the majesty of its Creator and to the whole passage of human history across its pages. The earth's crust bears the scars of abuse; its folds uncover the mysteries of regeneration and growth. We read its message in the language of color, shape, and distance. Its horizon is a metaphor; its seasonal journey an allegory. Like many good and important books, it sometimes surrenders its real message grudgingly. It beckons like a siren—tempting, rewarding, and, sometimes, destroying. It has often defied the rich who want to own it, the poor who want to till it for sustenance, and the wise who want to explain it.

Because the issues of land use and reform are key issues to the survival of humankind on earth, it seems necessary for the church to understand them—as it is important for the church to become engaged in all of the literally *vital* concerns of the earth's people. Some people question the ultimate value of church groups tackling complicated, multidisciplinary issues like that of land use. But without a mature, frank discussion of this and other social issues, little of true worth can be accomplished by the church, no matter how admirable its ideal goals may be. In fact, the genuine renewal of the spiritual dimension of life can actually be touched off by a discussion. As churchpeople come to a better understanding of their frame of reference—whatever it is—they can become more effective participants in the process of discussion and resolution.

The Episcopal Church, as well as other mainstream American churches, has been deeply involved in the debate on many of the great social issues of the twentieth century. They were deeply involved in movement against racism in the 1960s, in various aspects of family issues and concerns (abortion, divorce, population control), in the worldwide fight against hunger, in the struggle to help refugees of all kinds, and, most recently, in various aspects of the women's movement. This does not mean that Episcopalians always find themselves on the same side in every debate—nor do Methodists, Presbyterians, or Roman Catholics. But the fact of open debate in a Christian context is of great importance. For it is through discussion and debate, no matter which side one starts out on, that values are questioned and reshaped. The debate of Christians can produce amazing results.

The issues of land use and land reform raised in this book become more urgent with each passing year and each advance in technology. The battle to save the earth is not as "quiet" as it was when President Kennedy introduced Stewart Udall's book. As church groups of all kinds enter the discussion of this issue, they would be wise to heed these words of Udall in *The Quiet Crisis:*

> A land ethic for tomorrow should be as honest as Thoreau's *Walden,* and as comprehensive as the sensitive ecology. It should

stress the oneness of our resources and the live-and-help-live logic of the great chain of life. If, in our haste to "progress," the economics of ecology are disregarded by citizens and policy makers alike, the results will be an ugly America.

Notes on Organizing the Group

Let the Earth Bless the Lord is a resource book for adults. The sessions are informal, but there is a variety of material provided in the book to stimulate discussion and a wealth of material the participants will encounter in their everyday lives and bring to the group sessions. It would be wise for there to be established leadership—either an appointed or elected leader for the whole series or a rotating leadership with a leader elected for each session by the participants. A certain amount of the material is controversial—as are the issues it addresses—and a certain attempt will have to be made to keep the sessions orderly enough for the participants to profit from them.

The ideal length for these sessions would be 1½ to 2 hours. They could be scheduled after a Sunday morning church service in the traditional slot for adult education, or they could be scheduled as an evening series. They may be used, in modified form, at a weekend parish conference or by a cluster of parishes in your area; they may also be used with an ecumenical study group.

Make the series known to your congregation well in advance of the sessions. Have copies of the volume available in the church office or some other centrally-located place to be looked over before commitments to the group are made. It would be best to have a pre-series signing up session, short if necessary, a week prior to the beginning of the series. At this point, the person organizing the group should suggest that everyone read the Foreword and Introduction in advance of the first meeting. These sections set the tone for the rest of the series. The material in the Introduction dealing with the involvement of churches in the working out of social issues is an especially important understanding for group members.

Let the Earth Bless the Lord provides ten full session plans, each accompanied by substantial resource material. You might also wish to discuss, in your introductory pre-series meeting, how many sessions most of the potential group members would like to have. Ten sessions may be too long a commitment for adult groups in some churches. The leader or facilitator ought to be prepared to tell the assembled group what each of the sessions is about if they want to pick and choose. If the parish or congregation's response to the announcement of the series is substantial, it might be possible to run two groups concurrently with the materials provided. The two groups might choose to do some of the same sessions but come together to share learnings from sessions they didn't have in common.

The material which follows will be helpful to you as you make your plans to get your sessions moving. It is, of course, a suggested plan of procedure and should be adjusted to the special needs of your group.

Getting Started

Suggestions for the Person or Persons Who Will Lead the Sessions

- Announce the series in your parish bulletin. You might also consider posting clearly printed notices on church or parish bulletin boards.
- Provide sign up opportunities. If there is a parish bulletin, you could have a coupon attached to it that could be cut out, filled in, and dropped off at the church office—or mailed.
- Secure necessary resource materials that might help you, the leader or the organizer, in launching and carrying through the series. Your church or parish library or your local public library may have useful materials on adult education. A particularly helpful book to use in preparing a series of this kind has been published as part of The Church's Teaching Series. It is called *Equipping God's People: Basic Concepts for Adult Education* (Evans and Hayes, The Seabury Press, 1979).
- Once you know how many people there will be in the group, purchase books for each participant.
- If you are to be the leader or the person who gets the sessions started, read all of *Let Us Bless the Lord* before the first session.
- Plan a pre-series session to:
  —introduce the series and the issues it raises
  —suggest that everyone read the Foreword and the Introduction
  —choose a facilitator for the first session

—announce the time, date, and place of meeting
—decide on the most convenient time for everyone to meet and pass out contracts for group members if it is your choice to use them.

Session 1

LET THE EARTH
BLESS THE LORD

Bible Study and Discussion

Psalm 24 *

- Read and discuss Psalm 24; what does the Psalm tell us about creation, stewardship, and ownership?
- How do verses 3–6 help us to understand the relationship between the creator and the creation?
- Let your imagination be stirred and identify the "gates" and "doors" (v. 7) of contemporary society.

Moving Along

- Read and identify the issues in the opening essay, "Let the Earth Bless the Lord" (pp. 3–6).
- Has modern urban and technological life created a distance and disinterest in the land?
- Since the Old and New Testament times were agrarian in nature, does the Bible evoke specific guidelines for contemporary relations between nature and humanity?
- What does Ambrose mean by: "But avarice distributed the right of possession [of this earth]"?
- Just what do we celebrate at secular observances such as Thanksgiving? Is there a Biblical justification for these secular festivals? If so, what is it—be specific.
- Read Selections A and B (pp. 6–7). What does Henri Nouwen mean by "nature remains opaque"? Mr. Secretary Bergland answers his questioner quite bluntly; how would you respond to the same question?

---

*The New English Bible is the text referred to here and throughout *Let the Earth Bless the Lord*.

- In Selection C (from Archbishop Temple's *Christianity and Social Order*) (pp. 7–8), the author states: "But in any case it is for principles and not for precepts that Christians turn to the Old Testament." Discuss the implications of this statement.

Preparing for the Next Session

- Participants should be encouraged to read the essay "Burdens of Empire" (pp. 11–16) in Session 2.
  Since Kenya is the point of reference, independent research is encouraged.
- Identify a moderator for the next session who will be responsible for the discussion and the arrangements.
- Suggest that Psalm 107 (included in Session 2) be read before the next meeting.

Ending

- Read aloud:
  Isaiah 5:7–10
  Revelation 3:20
- Pause for silent meditation and reflection.
- Read together:
  Hymn 484 *

> Lift up your heads, ye mighty gates;
> Behold the King of glory waits!
> The King of kings is drawing near;
> The Saviour of the world is here.
>
> O blest the land, the city blest,
> Where Christ the ruler is confest!
> O happy hearts and happy homes
> To whom this King of triumph comes!
>
> Fling wide the portals of your heart;
> Make it a temple, set apart
> From earthly use for heaven's employ,
> Adorned with prayer and love and joy.
>
> Redeemer, come! I open wide
> My heart to thee: here, Lord, abide!

---

*The 1940 hymnal of The Episcopal Church is the text referred to here and throughout *Let the Earth Bless the Lord*.

Let me thy inner presence feel:
Thy grace and love in me reveal.

So come, my Sovereign; enter in!
Let new and nobler life begin;
Thy Holy Spirit guide us on,
Until the glorious crown be won.   Amen.

GEORGE WEISSEL, 1642, *based on Psalm 24*

· Read aloud:
  Prayer for Thanksgiving Day

  Almighty and gracious Father, we give you thanks for the fruits
  of the earth in their season and for the labors of those who harvest them. Make us, we pray, faithful stewards of your great
  bounty, for the provision of our necessities and the relief of all
  who are in need, to the glory of your Name; through Jesus Christ
  our Lord, who lives and reigns with you and the Holy Spirit, one
  God, now and for ever. *Amen.*

· Suggest that participants in the group write a prayer for the next
  session.

And at the Very End
Have the group assess the learning they have gained in the session.
· What did you learn?
· Identify any new insights you gained.
· What issues discussed in the session would you like to know more
  about?

Let the Earth Bless the Lord
Our relationship with the land and our concern for it are our life experiences. As an increasingly urban/suburban people, we Americans
find ourselves far removed from the world of our predecessors, whose
lives were visibly dependent upon the land's productivity. Our food
comes prepackaged, frozen, and often unrecognizable as originating
from the earth. Trees are transformed into homes, paper towels, news-
print, and even clothing. We rarely reflect on the source of our life's
physical sustenance or realize how fragile this source actually is.

However, today, in the midst of truly remarkable technological
achievements and complex land use systems, our land, the basis of
our existence, is in danger. Soil loss threatens hillsides in Asia, semi-

deserts spread across parts of Africa, and the corn and wheat belts of the United States are hard hit by wind and water erosion. Irrigated farm lands are increasingly burdened with saline residues that threaten to destroy the land's fertility. While American consumers face rapidly rising food prices, many American farmers are struggling in the face of mounting debt. Even as hunger stalks the globe, reflected in the eyes of gaunt and narrowed faces, valuable acres of fertile land are used for nonfood crops in Central America or turned into new housing developments in the valleys of California.

These matters are uncomfortable and shake us to the core. We are Christians; and the Gospel's call is to love our neighbor as ourself, to feed the hungry, and to care for God's creation. Beyond that, we cannot get away from profound and troubling questions: To whom does the earth belong? To us? To a nation? To individual owners? Or to God?

By examining what the Bible has to say about the land and its use, we will be better equipped to find answers to these questions. They are vital questions about faith and about the "good earth" that brings forth living things from its soil, affecting air and water and providing sustenance for living creatures. Our questions will also direct us to issues such as land use, land ownership rights, pollution, technology, urban migration, and farm systems. They concern Christians because our faith calls us not only to care for our neighbor, but also for creation. And it is in the very act of creation that our serach must begin.

Essential to the Genesis story is the truth that the "earth is the Lord's and the fullness thereof (Ps. 24:1)." This is nothing less than the remarkable affirmation that no man or woman has the ownership of the land without limitations. Such an understanding is jarring to a belief in the right to private property without external restrictions on that property's use. Limiting the right of ownership, especially of land, does not by itself dictate a particular system of land holdings; rather, it puts *all* human arrangements for land tenure under judgment of responsible stewardship.

What this all means is that no one has the right to use land in ways that despoil it. Because God is the ultimate owner and because succeeding generations have an equal right to the land's bounty, each temporal owner is responsible for maintaining the land's value. Indeed, one could argue that if one inhabits land that has been despoiled, one's stewardship includes rehabilitating the land for future generations. Clearly, this presents a different perspective than what most people are used to, yet it reflects the Biblical perspective: "No land shall be sold outright, because the land is mine, and you are coming into it as aliens and settlers (Lev. 25:23)."

Furthermore, God's ultimate ownership means that the land's use must include sharing and a concern for justice. This is apparent in the covenant that exists between God and the people of Israel: "The poor will always be with you in the land, and for that reason I command you to be open-handed with your countrymen, both poor and distressed, in your own land (Deut. 15:11)." From Jesus' teachings and life the essence of sharing was carried forward into the life of the church. Indeed, the writings of early Christians reflect this in dramatic and vivid terms: "God willed that this earth shall be the common possession of all and he offered its fruits to all. But avarice distributed the right of possession (St. Ambrose)."

Thus, not only the land itself, but also the fruits of the land belong to all. Without rigid legalism this means that there is a community responsibility to see that no one goes without basic necessities. Theories about how this is to be worked out may vary widely, but the Bible is clear about what it means to fail to share the land and its benefits. Covenant land was conditionally given from God with the understanding that it was to be part of a shared creation. The harsh words of the prophets reflect the sense of betrayal when the covenant of the land was abused for the benefit of a few: "Hear the word of the Lord, O Israel; for the Lord has a charge to bring against the people of the land: There is no good faith or mutual trust, no knowledge of God in the land. . . . (Hos. 4:1)."

Conditionality is part of the gift of land because the gift was given with warnings about its use. The covenant relationship that began with the exodus leading to the promised land is one of promise but also one of responsibility. It implies that the holders of the land will use it wisely and will be open to those in need. Jesus' teachings and actions likewise point to a humble attitude towards creation and reverence for the gifts of the land.

One important aspect that relates to God's creation and the need for sharing is the sense of a community's responsibility for its resource of land. Each community member has a stake and a claim in both the maintenance and the sustenance of the land. It is here that the meaning of being dispossessed is so vivid. In ancient Israel, predominantly rural, this was particularly visible in the lives of the landless. Beyond that particular loss, though, there is the broader meaning—those who are cut off from the land are also cut off from the fruits of creation.

Given the growing malaise in our own world, the specter of widespread hunger and environmental degradation, could it be that we are abusing land and its bounty? For the prophets, for Jesus, and for the early church, spiritual decay was linked with the unjust and inequitable uses of the land and of possessions (cf. Isa. 5:7–10).

In our own day, how do situations of hunger, soil loss, and pollution relate to each other, and to our spiritual journey? What does it mean that the land's harvest is used by a few landholders while many go hungry? Can we keep silent in the face of unsound farming practices done for the sake of immediate gain? These questions cannot be easily answered. Yet they pose a significant challenge for Christians seeking to hear and to answer God's call in the world today.

The challenge can be found both in examining the way land is used and in seeking to understand the forces that misuse the resources of creation. Such misuse is hardly new; neither is the responsibility to speak clearly God's concern in each generation: "Woe to those who devise wickedness and work evil upon their beds! When the morning dawns, they perform it, because it is in the power of their hands. They covet fields, and seize them; and houses, and take them away; they oppress a man and his house, a man and his inheritance (Mic. 2:1–2)."

Subsequent sections of this study will examine specific problems that are involved in our relationship to the land. All of these issues need to be seen in the light of the Biblical story of creation and God's continuing concern for all people. This study will challenge accepted ideas and attitudes. We hope that the readers will take up the challenge of the Biblical perspectives offered here and all they imply about working for just and sustainable land use systems on "this fragile earth our island home."

SELECTION A
from Henri Nouwen, *Clowning in Rome*

As long as we relate to the trees, the rivers, the mountains, the fields, and the oceans as properties we can maintain according to our real or fabricated needs, nature remains opaque and does not reveal to us its true being. When a tree is nothing but a potential chair, it ceases to tell us much about growth; when a river is only a dumping place for industrial wastes, it can no longer speak to us about movement; and when a flower is nothing more than a model for a plastic decoration, it has little to say about the simple beauty of life. When we relate to nature primarily as a property to be used, it becomes opaque—an opaqueness that in our society manifests itself as pollution. The dirty rivers, the smog filled skies, the strip mined hills, and the ravaged woods are sad signs of our false relationship with nature.

SELECTION B

Land and Farming in the United States

(from Charles Lutz, ed., *Farming the Lord's Land*)

November 26, 1978, "Face the Nation" (CBS), Secretary of Agriculture Robert Bergland and James Risser of the *Des Moines Register*

Mr. Risser: Mr. Secretary, there's quite a bit of evidence that the intensive agricultural production policies of the U.S. over the last couple of years are taking a tremendous toll in terms of soil erosion and depletion of water supplies. Can we continue our present intensive agricultural production without eventually wearing out our resources?

Mr. Bergland: We cannot. We're on a collision course with disaster. . . . Our water supplies are being reduced, we have whole watersheds where the ground water reserves are being depleted, and we have mined our soil. In fact, the erosion of America's farmland today is probably at a record rate, and this simply cannot go on.''

SELECTION C

from William Temple: *Christianity and Social Order*

The fundamental Biblical principle is that the earth—land—belongs to God; men enjoy the use of it, and this use may be so regulated as to ensure to particular families both security in that enjoyment and exclusive right to it. But this was to be so done as to ensure also that all members of the community shared in the enjoyment of some portion. There was to be no proletariat. There were thus to be rights of property, but they were rights shared by all, and were subject to the overruling consideration that God alone had ultimate ownership of the land, the families to whom it was allotted being His stewards. The Law of Jubilee, by which every fifty years alienated land reverted to its proper family, so that the permanent accumulation of a large estate in a single hand became impossible, rested on this basic principle of divine ownership. In the days of the Kings we find prophets denouncing such accumulations; so for example Isaiah exclaims: "Woe unto them that join house to house, that lay field to field, till there be no room, and ye be made to dwell alone in the midst of the land'' (Isaiah v. 8); and Micah: ''Woe to them that devise iniquity and work evil upon their beds! When the morning is light, they practice it, because it is in the power of their hand. And they covet fields and seize them; and houses, and take them away; and they oppress a man and his house, even a man and his heritage'' (Micah ii. 1, 2). And the evil here was not primarily economic, though that may have been involved. The evil was the denial of what Tertullian (*c.* 160–230) would call ''fellowship in property''—which seemed to him the natural result of unity in mind and spirit.

Of course the Mosaic legislation was designed for a community dependent on its own land. We are not; today there is a world-community in economic matters though not yet in political matters. But in any case it is for principles and not for precepts that Christians turn to the Old Testament. . . .

Session 2

BURDENS OF EMPIRE

Bible Study and Discussion

Psalm 107:33–43
Matthew 6:19–24

- Read and discuss Psalm 107, verses 33–43. You may want to suggest that the *whole* Psalm be read silently first and then verses 33–43 read aloud.
- Whereas Psalm 24 in Session 1 deals with the theme of *creation,* how does the psalmist view the Creator's *continued* role in nature?
- Read and discuss Matthew 6:19–24.
- What are the risks of wealth?
- What implications has this passage on the concept of humanity's stewardship and responsibility within the natural order?

Moving Along

- After reading the essay "Burdens of Empire" (pp. 11–16), can you identify any similarities between the colonization of Kenya and land appropriation and development in the United States, including Hawaii and Alaska?
- Discuss the problems of land reform—distribution, ownership, and maintenance.
- Read and discuss Selection A. Frame a response to the author's statement: "I would think of how the *sacadas* slave for every centavo, and how easily the rich man and the rich man's son squander the money they have not earned—and I saw the injustice of it all, and I began to understand why the communists are communists."
- Compare this quote from Milton's *Paradise Lost* (Book 1, ll. 679–684) with the quote from St. Ambrose in Session 1 (p. 1):

9

Mammon, the least erected spirit that fell
From Heaven; for even in Heaven his looks and thoughts
Were always downward bent, admiring more
The riches of Heaven's pavement, trodden gold,
Than aught divine or holy else enjoyed
In vision beatific.

Preparing for the Next Session

- The next session will focus on East Nepal. Participants may want to research and prepare material for sharing. Ask for volunteers.
- Call attention to the Scripture readings from the prophets Micah and Zephaniah. The writings of these prophets are short and are worth reading in full.
- Identify a moderator for the next session who will be responsible for the discussion and arrangements.

Ending

- Read aloud:
    Luke 12:32–34
    Acts 2:45
    Acts 4:34–37
- Pause for silent meditation and reflection.
- Read aloud:

Prayer for Stewardship of Creation

> O merciful Creator, your hand is open wide to satisfy the needs of every living creature: Make us always thankful for your loving providence; and grant that we, remembering the account that we must one day give, may be faithful stewards of your good gifts; through Jesus Christ our Lord, who with you and the Holy Spirit lives and reigns, one God, for ever and ever. *Amen.*

- If anyone has prepared a prayer, have that person share it with the group.
- Suggest participants write a prayer to be used at the next session.

And at the Very End

Have the group assess the learning they have gained in the session.

- What did you learn?
- Identify any new insights you gained.
- What issues discussed in the session would you like to know more about?

Burdens of Empire

"Growing food is one of the first things people learn when they come out of the trees."

The above statement, used by an American diplomat at a gathering of representatives of developing countries, reveals the misunderstanding inherent in many widely held views about agriculture. Even as few nations have the abundance of fertile land and temperate climate that the United States has, so do few of them have a history of overcoming the causes of hunger or poor productivity. Among the problems faced by developing countries are misapplication of temperate-zone technology, unique difficulties of tropical soils, lack of research in local agricultural needs, and misuse of natural resources—human and material. Along with all of these, many developing countries inherited from a colonial period farming systems that had radically altered traditional land use patterns. These colonial systems were developed for the convenience of the external ruling power, and this legacy has been a significant block to more effective rural development. The following essay will focus on the colonial history of Kenya. The British colonial rule in Kenya was far less harsh than, for example, that of the Belgians in Zaire or of the Portuguese in their African colonies. Thus this history can help reveal some normative patterns, as well as some unique ones, such as the existence of a large white settler group.

At the beginning of British rule in Kenya, the normal rural agricultural life pattern was that of peasant societies. The peasant systems were not egalitarian, nor were they communal in any idealized sense. There were, however, some general aspects that can be considered common. The land and livestock were owned by households, the labor was provided by the household, and land was seen as the essential form of capital. Entering into this situation, the British "alienated" or confiscated thousands of acres of prime farm land for the exclusive use of white settlers. This area, known as the White Highlands, was taken from the Kikuyu, the largest ethnic group in Kenya.

One of the immediate limitations placed upon African agriculture was the establishment of "reserves" for African landholders. This had several repercussions. Environmental stress increased in those areas where population pressures resulted in the greatest overuse of the land. Externally imposed boundaries placed strains on developing the land's productive capacity. Soil was worked without any rotation, and traditional conservation practices and the use of "shifting" agriculture were abandoned. As time passed, quality of the land declined. This would later lead to European criticism of the Africans for their "primitive" methods and abuse of the soil resources.

Another limitation on African agriculture was the strong bias that the colonial government showed towards the white settler farms. Peasant agriculture was neglected, even though it was a major part of the economy. There was no effort made to provide extension services for the peasants. Credit, technical support, access to markets by way of railroads or highways, and commercial encouragement were withheld from Africans.

The development of this settler economy, with its resultant land pressures and economic bias, had another result. Because of the overpopulation and declining productivity in the African land areas, there emerged a wage-earning group of Africans that found part or even most of its livelihood through employment on the large estates. Members of this group often faced the ambivalence of being rooted in their home villages yet having to migrate for work. Colonial taxation policies also intentionally induced Africans to work for wages in order to pay their taxes. Additionally, the taxation was regressive, with the poorer sectors, the Africans, seeing their meager wealth redistributed to the wealthier sector, the Europeans.

Psychologically, the African peasant was most immediately affected by the new situation relating to what had been traditional land areas. As one African chief said: "When someone steals your ox, it is killed and roasted and eaten. One can forget. When someone steals your land, especially if it is near-by, one can never forget. It is always there, its trees which were dear friends, its little streams. It is a bitter presence."

The continued flow of labor into the estates resulted in a gradual transition in the African economy. Tribal reserves were basically traditional in their economies, although that was to change eventually. Africans who worked as laborers lived a double economic existence of working part-time on the estates and then returning to a home plot for a modest harvest—one often nurtured and harvested by the women, children, and elderly left behind. This has become common in many areas of the "developing" world, as the rural poor find themselves trapped between low paying, part-time wage labor and the limitations of their own landholdings. The reasons for this type of dilemma vary from country to country; but an underlying cause has been the limitations placed on peasant agriculture, such as colonial regulations, taxation, heavy debts, plantations, lack of market access, which have created labor pools available to large capital enterprises. Since they are employed only when they are needed, many workers maintain ties to rural areas for times when jobs are not available.

The ascendancy of the settler's economic interests had other repercussions beyond those affecting the labor situation. Because the best lands had been set aside for the settlers, the Europeans had a major advantage in selling crops that peasants also sold. It did not end there. As was typical of colonial systems in general, the British colonial infrastructure of railroads, highways, and transport rating systems in Kenya was heavily biased towards European interests. Legitimate competition was never encouraged, and the policies of the colonial government had the effect of discouraging Africans from marketing those crops that placed them in competition with Europeans. These privileges were only furthered by the virtual monopoly enjoyed by the Europeans on access to credit, extension services, and veterinary services that existed in Kenya.

Eventually the strains in this system led to the violent uprising that has come to be called, without historical basis, "Mau Mau." This movement was based among the Kikuyu, who had suffered the most under the colonial land policies. What originated as the violence of landless Kikuyu against those Africans who had managed to hold on to some land spread into a challenge to the colonial system. After the imposition of police power during a period of "emergency," the British concluded that changes needed to be made in their Kenyan colony. Under the direction of the Swynnerton Plan, efforts were made to bring some Africans into the landholding system as the colony prepared for independence.

The basic structures of the landholding system were retained. Substituting Africans for Europeans did not meaningfully alter the direction that the system had taken since the early 1900s. Peasants generally remained unable to influence change in a coherent way. Practices that led to soil erosion and land degradation remained unchallenged. Nationalist movements that sought an end to colonial rule had a popular appeal, but they did not alter the land tenure system. As independence approached, the transfer of large tracts of land continued, but with only a small number of Africans as recipients.

Kenya's land redistribution programs both before and after independence are indicative of the difficulties of "land reform" programs.

There was never enough money to purchase as much land for redistribution as was needed. What occurred was either an expansion of membership in the large landholding group, or an increase in the holdings of a few Africans. For many of the rural poor, particularly those without land, life went on much as before. The flag had changed, but the system remained in many ways the same. Colin Leys describes the situation in his book, *Underdevelopment in Kenya:*

> The boundaries between the old "large-farm" sector and the "African land units," the one expatriate and capitalist, the other African and—at least till the 1950s—not only "peasant," but "poor peasant," were swiftly obliterated. In their place arose a new rural structure, predominantly occupied by Africans, with the foreign owned plantations and ranches still operating, much less visibly, though still more profitably, on the sidelines. It contained a system of graduations of acreage, capitalization, access to credit and know how and political protection which cut across the distinction between the former white highlands and the rest of the country. . . .
>
> At the top were some very large-scale individual land owners, some of them with farms purchased from Europeans, others with several hundred acres—not necessarily in one "parcel"—in the former reserves. These men were linked professionally, socially and economically to the foreign . . . enclave, borrowing from foreign banks, having accounts with foreign equipment companies, holding directorships in foreign companies. Their farms were mostly run by salaried managers. . . .
>
> At the bottom of the scale were the "peasant" masses, mostly now with freehold land titles, though little access to capital, extension services or other inputs—and—especially among the Kikuyu—a growing minority of landless laborers and squatters.

Land distribution policies following independence enabled thousands of Africans to gain holdings under the so-called "Million Acre Settlement Scheme." Half the acreage was allocated to small-holding families, the other half was available for purchase by more affluent Kenyans. In the end only a small percentage of the White Highlands was actually given over to small farmers. The remaining plantations stayed as they were, producing coffee, tea, and sisal, a form of hemp, for their old and new owners.

The colonial epoch radically shifted landholding and productive patterns in many developing countries. "Cash crops," such as coffee, tea, and rubber, were planted where food crops had been grown. Temperate-zone agricultural practices were introduced, leading to soil erosion, hardening of soils, and "desertification" in tropical regions. Taxation and labor policies impoverished the rural populations and increased landlessness in many regions. One of the most radical colonial programs occurred in Zimbabwe, formerly Rhodesia. The following discussion is offered by Robin Palmer in *Roots of Rural Poverty in Central and Southern Africa:*

> It is against . . . a background of racial hostility that one needs to look at the impoverishment of the African peasantry in Rhodesia. The remarkable prosperity enjoyed by many Shona farmers in the early years of the century was brought to an end by a combination of factors. Primarily, African farmers faced the full blast of competition from heavily subsidized European farmers while simultaneously being away from easy access to markets, a process greatly facilitated by the work of the 1914–15 Native Reserves Commission, which reduced the reserves by a million acres and took from them much of the best land within easy reach of the main centers. In addition, Africans were confronted with an ever increasing number of costly dues. . . .

Given the sad history of most developing countries, it is crucial that we increase our awareness of all possible impediments to more productive and equitable agricultural systems. Analyzing the effects of colonial policies is an important step toward achieving that awareness. There are additional steps, which are discussed in other parts of these essays. What is essential is the realization that whatever the problems, they are soluble and not the result of some natural phenomenon or cultural inferiority. With this realization comes a perspective different from present viewpoints that are often at odds with reality.

The essential situation found in Kenya—the expropriation of the best farming land, the use of this land for cash crops for export, the displacement of peasants, the differential treatment of large landholders vs. small peasant landholders—may be found in other developing countries that were formerly colonies. Gunnar Myrdal provides one example of such a viewpoint in *Asian Drama:*

> Contrary to the prevalent assumption, the ratio of man to land is not strikingly high [in South Asia] compared with other parts of the world. The number of inhabitants per unit of cultivated land is comparable to the European average. It is half that of China and of course, much lower than that of Japan. What really

distinguishes South Asia is the very low output per unit of farm land and per unit of work on that land.

While the situation in South Asia differs from the situation in Africa in many ways, there are similarities in the histories of these regions, in terms of both disruptive colonial policies and applications of inappropriate technological changes. Learning about these areas and their histories makes it possible to envision more just and sustainable agricultural systems for the present and the future. Indeed, Kenya today is not particularly backward. Many industries are prospering, certain areas of agriculture are doing well, and social conflict is muted. Nevertheless, there are disturbing signs: erosion of soil, rivers running red with rich earth, the plowing up of grasslands, and growing migration to the cities where there are not enough jobs. The pattern set during the colonial period, for better and for worse, has helped shape Kenya's present and will affect its future.

SELECTION A
LAND OWNERSHIP
by Arsenio Jesena

There were 200 of us—men, women and children staying in two adjoining *quartels*. There was not a single toilet. There was only one source of water—an old pump. Here everyone did his or her washing, bathing, laundering. We had no blankets, no mosquito nets. For food, three times a day we were served rice—the cheapest, driest, coarsest, most unappetising I have ever tasted. Many of the grains were unhusked, and there were pieces of gravel to be found among the grains of rice. Rough rice and dry fish, that was all. No liquid, no vegetable, a diet which gave no delight and no strength. Yet strength is needed for the *socada's* (migrant workers) work. At 3.30 a.m., the lights come on, and by 5.00 a.m. the *socadas* have trudged, barefoot, through the one kilometre which separates the canefields from the *quartels*. The *socada's* work is cutting and loading. This is easier said than done.

The work of cutting is monotonous—the same endless bending of the entire body, the same strong cutting strokes of the *expading* with one hand, the same grasping and jerking and piling up of the sugarcane by the other hand. This work is also very exacting. It saps away one's strength in a very short time. Added to this is the discomfort of wearing thick, close-necked, long-sleeved denims (to protect oneself against cuts and rashes from the *gilok* and the leaves) under the heat of the burning sun. But the *sacada* must continually keep on working, since, if he is to eat, he is supposed to cut tons of sugar cane.

The *sacada* must now load the sugarcane. He bends down, grapples with his pile of 25 to 35 canes, and then, under this heavy burden, navigates his way through the field to the railroad tracks where he dumps his load into the *bagon*. Then the *sacada* goes through the whole process again and again until all the sugar cane he has cut is completely loaded into the railway cars.

Sometimes when I could no longer raise my arm for another cutting stroke of the *espading*, or when, after carrying a heavy load to the *bagon* I would, from sheer exhaustion, just sit down on the ground. I would look up and see the *sacadas* still at work—some of them younger than my students, some of them older than my father, carrying twice the load I could carry. I could not help but be struck by a terrible contrast—for I would think of the *sacadas*, who work so hard, and receive so little, and I would think of my students in the Ateneo, who do so little, and receive so much. I would think of how the *sacadas* slave for every centavo, and how easily the rich man and the rich man's son squander the money they have not earned—and I saw the injustice of it all, and I began to understand why the communists are communists.

As the day ends, the *sacadas* slowly drag their way back through the cane-fields and the dusty roads to the *quartels* where they know they will be met by the same unappetising food. As they walk on, a cloud of dust would be kicked up by an occasional Mercedes-Benz zooming past as the *hacendero* hurries to an appointment in Bacolod. As the *sacadas* near the quartels they see the children they love—dirty and tattered clothing, children who like them would inevitably fit into the perpetual cycle of ignorance and hard work. Some of those who have gone home earlier would be sitting about doing nothing, one of them perhaps strumming a guitar, but giving forth that music peculiar to the *sacadas* which always has a plaintive note of melancholy and despair.

No, the *sacadas* are not happy as they trudge back from their back-breaking work. And to think—for most of them, life would be like this for 30, 40 years—until they are too old to swing an *espading*. And so, to escape, if only for a moment, from a lifetime of much labour and little reward, some of them search out the *tuba* vendor, get drunk, and fall into the temporary peace that sleep can give.

But not all the *sacadas* sleep at once. In the darkness of the night many of us would huddle around and listen to each one open his heart and recount his personal tragedy. And these tough, hardened men—I actually saw them cry! And some cried like little children. And no word of ours could stop their sobbing and their tears.

Session 3

THE DILEMMA
OF
LAND REFORM

Bible Study and Discussion

Micah 1:3–10
Zephaniah 3:11–20

- Read and discuss the passages from Micah and Zephaniah.
- What impression does Micah give you concerning God's continued participation in history?
- How do you interpret Micah's vision that the "wound cannot be healed" (v.9)? Can you associate this with a contemporary view of world problems?
- What hope do you find in the reading from Zephaniah?

Moving Along

- Discuss the "syndrome of agricultural indebtedness," as summarized in the essay (p. 21). You may have to diagram the process in order to identify the major ingredients.
- The key word in this session and in the previous one is "sustainable." Identify the structures in both Kenya and East Nepal that (a) sustain the problem and (b) are necessary to sustain any solution.
- Read Selections A and B (pp. 23–27) from the Presidential Commission on World Hunger and the report for the president by the State Department and Council on Environmental Quality. What do they say about advancing solutions through the "political will"?
- Read Selection C: "Doomsday Postponed" (pp. 27–30), and compare it with the two Scripture readings.

Preparing for the Next Session

- Identify a moderator for the next session.
- The next session, entitled "Land Ownership," may need serious

preparation. Advance reading of the lead article will be of great assistance. For preparation in depth, read Wendell Berry's *The Unsettling of America* (New York: Avon Books, 1978).

Ending

- Read aloud:
  Psalm 96
- Pause for silent meditation and reflection.
- Read (or sing):
  Hymn 319

> Joy to the world! the Lord is come:
>> Let earth receive her King;
> Let every heart prepare him room,
>> And heaven and nature sing.
>
> Joy to the world! the Saviour reigns:
>> Let men their songs employ,
> While fields and floods, rocks, hills and plains,
>> Repeat the sounding joy.
>
> No more let sins and sorrows grow,
>> Nor thorns infest the ground;
> He comes to make his blessings flow
>> Far as the curse is found.
>
> He rules the world with truth and grace,
>> And makes the nations prove
> The glories of his righteousness,
>> And wonders of his love.

ISAAC WATTS, 1719

- Share the prayers composed by the members of the group.
- Read aloud:
  Prayer for the Future of the Human Race

O God our heavenly Father, you have blessed us and given us dominion over all the earth: Increase our reverence before the mystery of life; and give us new insight into your purpose for the human race, and new wisdom and determination making provision for its future in accordance with your will through Jesus Christ our Lord.

And at the Very End

Have the group assess the learning they have gained in the session.

- What did you learn?
- Identify any new insights you gained.
- What issues discussed in the session would you like to know more about?

The Dilemma of Land Reform: A Case of East Nepal

Blame for the widespread poor use and unjust distribution of land in the developing countries cannot always be attributed to the domination of foreign nations or large corporations over small-scale societies. Although there are numerous examples of modern land reform efforts to combat the devastating effects of colonial manipulation of land ownership and agricultural production patterns in the third world, a case from eastern Nepal illustrates the struggle of an indigenous group to preserve their traditional system of land tenure in the face of domination by another group, who, although historically and culturally alien, are, nevertheless, present as immigrants within their community.

The setting is in the District of Ilam, bound on the east by Sikkim and the Darjeeling district of West Bengal, which is characterized by Himalayan mountainsides that require steep terracing for the cultivation of rice, millet, and maize within a subsistence economy. Home for a number of tribal peoples of Mongolian background, the area was united mainly by force under a Hindu dynasty into what became the Kingdom of Nepal in the latter half of the eighteenth century. In the wake of the conquest, a large number of Hindus migrated into the tribal areas, creating a multiethnic society that became engaged in two seemingly opposite tendencies: conflict and interdependence. The Limbus, the predominant ethnic group in the easternmost portion of Nepal, describe the crux of the conflict like this: "The Hindus came as immigrant settlers and, ever since, have tried by fair means and foul, to 'eat' our land."

A Hindu–tribal land struggle is not unique to Nepal; there are many accounts of Hindu settlers entering tribal areas in India and succeeding in acquiring large stretches of the indigenous tribes' land, supported by a code of law. In most cases in South Asia, the tribes are regarded as the backward, the exploited, and the dispossessed, while the Hindus are those who exploit and dispossess them—more powerful economically, politically, and educationally.

The evolution of land tenure systems in the Limbuan district stands as a very interesting exception to the usual pattern of clear-cut domination of one community by another. Until 1964, when a comprehensive series of land reform measures was implemented throughout the entire kingdom, the government of Nepal followed a policy in Ilam that, for the most part, favored the maintenance of the traditional land tenure system. With the exception of those belonging to the Limbu, the government authorities had brought all tribal lands under a uniform system of tenure, known as "raikar," a state landlordism under which a person's rights to utilization and transfer of land are recognized by the state so long as taxes are paid. Traditionally, all tribal groups had held land under a customary form of tenure known as "kipat," under which a person obtained rights to land by virtue of his membership in a series of kin groups of patrilineal descent. The conversion of these lands to raikar led to their alienation to Hindu groups. The kipat system was not totally abolished in Ilam; however, legislation did reduce the area held under kipat by the Limbus, and the old and new systems existed side by side. The Hindu–tribal relationships continued to be strained as their interdependence increased; the confrontation over land was not easily resolved, even when total domination of one group over the other was curtailed.

The increased population in the area and the lack of uncultivated arable land meant that the economic obligations of Limbu households could only be met by mortgaging kipat lands to Hindu creditors, who assumed the use of the land pending repayment of the loans. The result was the familiar syndrome of agricultural indebtedness: As more and more lands were pledged to raise nonproductive capital, the Limbus gradually lost the means to repay their debts and resume their lands. Furthermore, the Brahmans, the highest caste among the Hindus and the most numerous and literate, controlled the majority of raikar headmanships. They acquired many lands which had previously belonged to Limbus under kipat tenure, thereby becoming the chief source of credit and tenancy for the Limbus. Additionally, the Limbus were often forced into the position of serving as hired laborers on the land they owned but could not afford to cultivate for themselves. The economic foundation and political hierarchy that had preserved some power for the Limbus continued to erode, worsened by a new system of tax collection that allowed the Hindus to pay taxes directly to the treasury office, bypassing the traditional tribal collectors and making corruption even easier.

However, in 1901, the government passed a decree that prohibited the permanent alienation of kipat land, and the Limbus were granted more flexibility in seeking credit. The pressures on raikar land grew steadily, and Brahmans were forced to compete for access to kipat land; the Limbus, then, were in a position to demand interest-free loans against the security of pledged lands. Additionally, in the aftermath of the First World War, the Limbus profited from their opportunities to earn cash income from military service (the famed Gurkha regiments). The growth of government services since 1951 has stimulated economic activity even further. Increased incomes slowed down the rate of kipat pledging and greatly reduced the Limbu dependence on the Brahmans, who still dominated access to Limbu lands. The two groups who never benefitted from this paradoxical relationship were the landless Limbus—those without proper descent and unable to afford raikar lands, and women—even the minimal rights to land held by unmarried daughters were hedged by many male-dominated stipulations. These two groups were victims even within a system that reserved some advantage for the exploited.

In 1968, the central government legislated the sale of kipat land; and the Limbu's persistent struggle to defend their ancestral system of tenure against the dominance of the alien privileged caste was halted by a well-intentioned nationwide policy.

Whether it is the scars of a colonial legacy in Kenya or the Hindu caste system superimposed on indigenous hill people in Nepal, the barriers to a just and sustainable land system are immense in the absence of a strong political will towards that goal. One wonders about the possibility for such a will to exist.

SELECTION A
A QUESTION OF WILL

Eliminating at least the worst aspects of hunger requires commitment on the part of both developed and developing countries. To date, neither the developed nor the developing countries have given top priority to alleviating hunger or investing in agriculture in the poor countries. Domestic political problems, national security questions, industrial development, and improving armies and cities have often attracted more attention and resources in the developing countries than investment in agriculture, health care or education. Moreover, policies that have emphasized "modernizing" the economy rather than assur-

Summary of the report of the Presidential Commission on World Hunger (1980).

ing that the benefits of development reach the poorest—and hungriest—people have often caused the gap between rich and poor to widen, rather than to narrow.

The rich industrialized countries have also not paid adequate attention to the alleviation of hunger. In setting their policies toward the developing world, the United States and other developed countries have not given the elimination of hunger a high priority and have too often been guided by short-term security and political concerns. As a result, they have often paid more attention to training local military personnel than to educating teachers, farmers, scientists, economists and health care specialists.

While more countries are talking about hunger and meeting the basic needs of the world's people, words have not yet been translated into decisive action. Action must begin immediately both to alleviate hunger in the short-run and to build a world in which there is no hunger. While this requires commitment—and, in some cases, political, economic and social reform—by the developing countries themselves, the Presidential Commission on World Hunger has examined what the United States can do to assist in the process.

SELECTION B
REPORT URGES GLOBAL ACTION ON RESOURCES
by Philip Shabecoff
Reprinted from *The New York Times,* July 24, 1980.

Time is running out for international action to prevent a starving, overcrowded, polluted, resource-poor world, according to a report for President Carter prepared by the State Department and Council on Environmental Quality.

The report, which President Carter ordered three years ago, was described by Administration officials as the most exhaustive and well-documented study ever produced of long-term changes in the world's population, natural resources and environment and the implications of those changes for populations and public policy.

In a letter transmitting the report to the President, the authors warn that they have found "the potential for global problems of alarming proportions by the year 2000," adding, "Environmental, resource and population stresses are intensifying and will increasingly determine the quality of human life on our planet."

The report itself concludes: "If present trends continue, the world in 2000 will be more crowded, more polluted, less stable ecologically, and more vulnerable to disruption than the world we live in now."

No recommendations for dealing with the predicted problems are made in the report other than urging that the nations of both the industrial and developing worlds, with the United States taking the lead, start now to undertake "determined new initiatives."

The report had been scheduled to be made public tomorrow by the White House, but publication was advanced when an embargo on its release was broken today by the Knight-Ridder newspapers.

As a result of the report, President Carter will establish a new Cabinet-level "Task Force on Global Resources and the Environment" under the chairmanship of Gus Speth, chairman of the Council on Environmental Quality, to insure "high priority attention is given to important global resource, population and environment problems."

In an interview, Mr. Speth said that while the 800-page report presented no startling new findings, "it is in many respects important and, indeed, unique." He continued:

"It is, for example, the first time this Government or any government has made an effort to project the trends in all of these crucial areas at once. It is the most highly detailed and quantified study of these trends and their interrelationship ever made. And it provides the basis for major strides forward for domestic and international policy."

"We have to understand that these are absolutely crucial issues we must address for humanitarian and security reasons," he added.

Asserting that "the world in 2000 will be different from the world today in important ways," the report presents these forecasts on population, income, resources and the environment:

Population

There will be little slowdown in the rapid growth of the world's population, which will grow from 4 billion in 1975 to 6.35 billion in 2000. The vast majority of the added populace will be in the poorer, less developed countries.

There will also be major shifts of population from rural to urban areas. Mexico City, with a population of 11 million in 1975, is projected to have 31.6 million by 2000.

Income

While the output of goods and services is expected to grow more rapidly in many less-developed countries than in the industrialized nations, the gap between rich and poor will increase because high population growth rates will keep per capita income low in the poorer countries.

While per-capita gross national product is expected to reach $8,000 annually in 1975 dollars in the industrialized countries and $14,212 in the United States, in the less developed countries per capita gross national product will average less than $600 a year, the report states.

Food

Assuming no deterioration as a result of climate changes or other factors, world food production is expected to increase by about 90 percent from 1970 to 2000 and per-capita production nearly 15 percent in the same period. However, most of the increased food consumption will be in countries where diets already are adequate or better. Individual food consumption in South Asia, Africa and the Middle East will hardly grow at all and in some cases will decline below present levels.

Meanwhile, the price of food in constant dollars is expected to double within 20 years largely because of the rising price of petroleum used in agricultural production.

Fisheries

The world fish harvest, an important source of protein, leveled off in 1970 and is not expected to increase by much, if at all, by the year 2000. Despite increased fish farming and the gathering of nontraditional marine species, such as Arctic krill, pollution and overfishing are likely to keep the harvest at no more than current levels.

Forests

Deforestation of the world is proceeding rapidly and per-capita supplies of growing stocks of wood is expected to decline 47 percent worldwide by 2000. The shortage will be critical in cultures that depend on firewood for fuel.

Water

Regional water shortages, already serious in many parts of the world, are likely to become worse 20 years from now in the face of increasing demand for water for human consumption, irrigation and new systems of energy production.

Energy

In the 1990's, world oil production will reach maximum capacity and prices will continue to rise as demand also increases sharply. The burden of energy prices will fall most heavily on the less developed countries.

Nonfuel Minerals

There is no projection that any mineral resources will be exhausted by 2000, but prices will rise sharply as will prices for most commodities in a resource-scarce world.

Environment

The report says that perhaps the most serious environmental problem over the next 20 years will be "an accelerating deterioration and loss of the resources essential for agriculture," including the loss of crop land to erosion and deserts as well as the increasing urbanization of lands now devoted to growing food. The use of pesticides and other chemicals, while increasing yields, now present a broad range of serious environmental threats to crop lands and people.

The heavy use of chemicals also will mean spreading water pollution. Increasing salinity from excessive irrigation is also likely to threaten water supplies.

Despite progress in reducing air pollution, the quality of air is expected to worsen, in the developing as well as industrialized countries, as increased amounts of oil, coal and other hydrocarbon fuels are burned.

One result will be an increase in the amount of carbon monoxide in the air, which many scientists believe will raise the world's temperature with disastrous results. Also to be expected is more acid rain, which is believed to destroy wildlife in freshwater lakes and damage cropland. Increased ozone in the air could sharply increase the incidence of skin cancer and damage food crops.

Finally, the report says, "the world faces an urgent problem of loss of plant and animal genetic resources" through the accelerating extinction of species.

Guide to Governments

The authors of the study said that public policy in this country and abroad was starting to address some of these problems. They also emphasized that the report was not a prediction of what would actually be the situation in the world in the year 2000 but rather a call and a guide to governments to adopt policies to avert the predicted trends.

"This is not a council of despair," Mr. Speth said in the interview. "We have an opportunity because of this timely warning to address these issues before it is too late."

One of the major lessons to be learned from the report, he said, is that "it is a mistake to view economic, development and environmental protection as antagonistic."

The focus of the new task force formed by President Carter today, Mr. Speth said, will be to "build a consensus" in this country and internationally on the course of action that must be taken to deal with the threats described by the report.

SELECTION C
DOOMSDAY POSTPONED
by Stewart McBride
Reprinted from *The Christian Science Monitor,* August 26, 1980.

Paul R. Ehrlich could never be called an optimist, but his pessimism has lifted a little. Twelve years ago, Stanford University's renowned population biologist and author of a 1968 best seller, "The Population Bomb," was solemnly warning: Curb population and stop destroying natural resources—or the planet is doomed. Today, he finds the problems just as severe, but the solutions more likely.

A few weeks ago on Stanford's Jasper Ridge Biological Preserve, where Dr. Ehrlich is continuing his famous 21-year study of the checkerspot butterfly, he paused to discuss his cautious new optimism.

"There's good reason to be optimistic," Professor Ehrlich says. "In 1965, when I talked about the chance of controlling the US population, I said we would be lucky to get to a net reproductive rate of 1 by the year 1992. Sociologists told me it would take 20 to 30 years of hard work to get the nation's average family size down from three to two [children].

"It turned out we were dead wrong. Society was ready for it and it took about three years. In the last 15 years, the environment has become a major political issue. Society can change its ways very fast when it sees reason to. But if you extrapolate today's behavior with no change into the future, we're doomed. The hope is that our behavior will change.

"Eight years ago the Brazilian point of view was, 'You and the rich countries have messed up your environment for fun and profit. Now it's our turn,' and they launched themselves on the destruction of the Amazon Basin. Now there's been almost a complete turnaround. The attitudinal change is there almost globally."

At the root of the environmental problem, according to Ehrlich, is that most Americans—especially the economists and politicians—still believe that if air and water pollution is stopped, their problems would be over.

Not so, Ehrlich says. What's missing is any understanding of what he calls the "free public services" provided to human beings by an intricate, but often delicate, network of ecological systems.

"It doesn't take much to change the entire system," the biologist explains. "It's just like a pistol with a six-ounce pull on the trigger. The last 1/100th of an ounce may tip the balance and the gun fires. People now calculate that a single-degree change in the global temperature, put there by carbon dioxide from fossil fuels, could entrain weather change which would devastate agriculture and lead to famines that could kill a billion or more people."

"You've got to remember," he says, "that the ecological machinery is composed of tiny individual species that we are pushing one after another to extinction, without the slightest understanding of the role they play in maintaining us. People are generally agreed that it's not appropriate to whip your horse to death or torture your dog. The question is, how far are they willing to extend that right to other organisms.

"Claude Lévi-Strauss, the great French anthropologist, once said—and he's quite correct—that the lowliest species of bug is a marvel of magnitude more fantastic than something like the Mona Lisa, as far as beauty, intimacy, and irreplaceability."

Americans who consider the idea of ecological disaster rather remote should consult the history books, Ehrlich says. The world is littered with the remains of civilizations unable to maintain their ecological equilibrium.

"The Romans went under, in part, because they destroyed the forests and screwed up their agriculture. In the Tigris and Euphrates Valleys, there's the remainder of a civilization that failed to manage its irrigation. In Cambodia is the remains of a Khmer civilization that has lost the game of tropical agriculture," says Ehrlich.

Americans' false sense of security is largely attributable to a "super science view of the world"—however serious our problem, they believe technology will find a way out. But according to Professor Ehrlich, the world can no longer bulldoze its way to a solution, partly because science and technology—the popular panaceas—are part of the problem.

"If you asked me right now, 'Has science been a net benefit or a net harm to mankind?' I would have to say, 'I don't know.' So far it's done about as much harm as it's done good. Maybe a little more harm than good. Americans are part of the lucky group, but most people in the world are living considerably more miserable lives than they lived six or seven thousand years ago. We are the most vulnerable population the world has ever seen. We're more crowded. We have more undernourished people than have ever lived before," he says.

Often mankind has to be driven to "the edge" before human behavior can be changed. The problem is that the "edge is getting steeper," the biologist says. Referring specifically to America's tendency to put "all our eggs in the nuclear [energy and defense] basket," he laments: "Sooner or later either a large city will disappear under a terrorist bomb, or there'll be a nuclear war, or a full-scale meltdown, at which point everybody will say, 'OK, no more nuclear power.' But if you've got to be taught a lesson with a war that wipes out 99 percent of humanity and leaves a few scattered groups in the Southern Hemisphere barely struggling on the edge of existence, that's a high price to pay for learning."

Ecologists, he adds, have been warning for years that unless the United States changes its gluttonous ways, it will find itself on the brink of war over scarce world resources. The present crisis in Iran and Afghanistan is precisely that nightmare, according to the professor. He believes Zbigniew Brzezinski, President Carter's national-security adviser, would risk getting into a war that could "possibly end the world, in order to gain access to the last 20 or 30 years of Arab oil. The people who run the country think it's worth going to war over, rather than driving smaller cars."

Next to the possibility of war, the danger that concerns Dr. Ehrlich most is economic growth.

"Economists think that the whole world is just a market system, and that free goods are infinitely supplied. They are a discipline built on transparent mistakes, from the point of view of a physicist or a biologist.

"Economists are probably the most dangerous single profession on earth, because they are listened to. They continue to whisper in the ears of politicians, all kinds of nonsense. Everybody feels that the economic system is what dominates human affairs, when actually the economic system is hopelessly embedded in the physical and environmental systems. Economists say it's jobs or the environment, when actually if you don't treat the environment right, there will be no jobs."

Ehrlich's one-word explanation for the United States' "environmental myopia" is "politics." Politicians, he says, have difficulty seeing beyond the next election. "As Churchill or somebody once stated, democracy is a stinking, inefficient system; it just happens to be the best we've got."

While the biologist has no desire for a benevolent dictator, he believes the US needs leaders with backbone to pull it out of the present environmental nose dive.

"In some countries," says Ehrlich, "the government can say, 'If you can't build a car that gets 50 miles to the gallon you won't be allowed to build any.' Instantly you have the 50-mile-a-gallon car. I can recall very clearly when we went into the Second World War we tooled up for that in a matter of a year or so. We changed the entire economy. Everybody behaved and pitched in. If you skipped the war itself, the experience was completely un-traumatic.

"The sorts of environmental measures that need to be taken today will not be popular, because relatively few people understand the urgency of the situation. When people begin to sense the urgency, almost anything goes. That's where my hope lies."

Session 4

LAND OWNERSHIP

Bible Study and Discussion

Psalm 65
- *Revelation 4:11; 5:9–10, 13*
- Read and discuss the Biblical passages.
- Both Scriptural passages acclaim the mighty workings of God, and both record the human response. In the light of these readings, discuss the theological concepts of "redemption" and "salvation."

Moving Along

- What is meant by "capital intensive farming"?
- Reread Henri Nouwen's statement in the Session 1 (p. 6) and compare it with Wendell Berry's on pages 47–54.
- If it is interdependent, can humans have "dominion" over one part of nature?
- Make a list of your household goods, especially food, which have been imported; try to identify the country of origin.
- After reading the article "The Destruction of Black Wolf," (pp. 54–58), discuss what you think Ms. Giardina means by "straining to see the day when the children of God come into their own"?

Preparing for the Next Session

- List the issues you did not have time to discuss in this session and explore ways of dealing with them at a future meeting.
- Identify the moderator for the next session.

Ending

- Read aloud:
  The Song of the Three verses 35–65
  (found in the Apocrypha)

A Song of Creation *Benedicite, omnia opera Domini*
Song of the Three Young Men, 35–65

Invocation

Glorify the Lord, all you works of the Lord,
  praise him and highly exalt him for ever.
In the firmament of his power, glorify the Lord,
  praise him and highly exalt him for ever.

I   The Cosmic Order

Glorify the Lord, you angels and all powers of the Lord,
  O heavens and all waters above the heavens.
Sun and moon and stars of the sky, glorify the Lord,
  praise him and highly exalt him for ever.

Glorify the Lord, every shower of rain and fall of dew,
  all winds and fire and heat.
Winter and summer, glorify the Lord,
  praise him and highly exalt him for ever.

Glorify the Lord, O chill and cold,
  drops of dew and flakes of snow.
Frost and cold, ice and sleet, glorify the Lord,
  praise him and highly exalt him for ever.

Glorify the Lord, O nights and days,
  O shining light and enfolding dark.
Storm clouds and thunderbolts, glorify the Lord,
  praise him and highly exalt him for ever.

II   The Earth and its Creatures

Let the earth glorify the Lord,
  praise him and highly exalt him for ever.
Glorify the Lord, O mountains and hills,
  and all that grows upon the earth,
  praise him and highly exalt him for ever.

Glorify the Lord, O springs of water, seas, and streams,
  O whales and all that move in the waters.
All birds of the air, glorify the Lord,
  praise him and highly exalt him for ever.

Glorify the Lord, O beasts of the wild,
  and all you flocks and herds.
O men and women everywhere, glorify the Lord,
  praise him and highly exalt him for ever.

III   The People of God

Let the people of God glorify the Lord,
    praise him and highly exalt him for ever.
Glorify the Lord, O priests and servants of the Lord,
    praise him and highly exalt him for ever.

Glorify the Lord, O spirits and souls of the righteous,
    praise him and highly exalt him for ever.
You that are holy and humble of heart, glorify the Lord,
    praise him and highly exalt him for ever.

Doxology

Let us glorify the Lord: Father, Son, and Holy Spirit;
    praise him and highly exalt him for ever.
In the firmament of his power, glorify the Lord,
    praise him and highly exalt him for ever.

- Pause for silent meditation and reflection.
- Read (or sing):
    Hymn 347

Alleluia! sing to Jesus!
    His the scepter, his the throne:
Alleluia! his the triumph,
    His the victory alone;
Hark! the songs of peaceful Sion
    Thunder like a mighty flood;
Jesus out of every nation
    Hath redeemed us by his blood.

Alleluia! not as orphans
    Are we left in sorrow now;
Alleluia! he is near us,
    Faith believes, nor questions how:
Though the cloud from sight received him,
    When the forty days were o'er,
Shall our hearts forget his promise,
    "I am with you evermore"?

Alleluia! Bread of Heaven,
    Thou on earth our food, our stay!
Alleluia! here the sinful
    Flee to thee from day to day:
Intercessor, friend of sinners,
    Earth's Redeemer, plead for me,

Where the songs of all the sinless
  Sweep across the crystal sea.

Alleluia! King eternal,
  Thee the Lord of lords we own:
Alleluia! born of Mary,
  Earth thy footstool, heaven thy throne:
Thou within the veil hast entered,
  Robed in flesh, our great High Priest:
Thou on earth both Priest and Victim
  In the eucharistic feast.

Alleluia! sing to Jesus!
  His the scepter, his the throne;
Alleluia! his the triumph,
  His the victory alone;
Hark! the songs of holy Sion
  Thunder like a mighty flood;
Jesus out of every nation
  Hath redeemed us by his blood. Amen.

w. c. dix, 1866

• Recite responsively (moderator and participants):

Human Nature

Q. What are we by nature?
A. We are part of God's creation, made in the image of God.

Q. What does it mean to be created in the image of God?
A. It means that we are free to make choices: to love, to create,
   to reason, and to live in harmony with creation and with
   God.

Q. Why then do we live apart from God and out of harmony
   with creation?
A. From the beginning, human beings have misused their freedom and made wrong choices.

Q. Why do we not use our freedom as we should?
A. Because we rebel against God, and we put ourselves in the
   place of God.

Q. What help is there for us?
A. Our help is in God.

Q. How did God first help us?
A. God first helped us by revealing himself and his will,

through nature and history, through many seers and saints, and especially through the prophets of Israel.

- Read aloud:

Prayer For Knowledge of God's Creation

Almighty and everlasting God, you made the universe with all its marvelous order, its atoms, worlds, and galaxies, and the infinite complexity of living creatures: Grant that, as we probe the mysteries of your creation, we may come to know you more truly, and more surely fulfill our role in your eternal purpose; in the name of Jesus Christ our Lord.

- Share prayers written by participants.

And at the Very End
Have the group assess the learning they have gained in the session.
- What did you learn?
- Identify any new insights you gained.
- What issues discussed in the session would you like to know more about?

Land Ownership
Land is life. Our lives, whether we are homeowners in southern California or peasant farmers in Guatemala, are intimately connected to the life of the land; and the relationship is one of mutual dependence and influence. The significance of land in our own society, the United States, can be traced to our Constitution, which embodies the right of every citizen to own land as one of the fundamental tenets of democracy. In our early history this meant the glorification of the independent farmer, the "Jeffersonian ideal"; yet with the growth of industrialization and the rule of the market economy, this ideal has become more a dream than a reality, and issues of land ownership rights are the subject of increasingly numerous legal battles from city councils to the U.S. Supreme Court. How can our deeply rooted connections to the land be understood? How can we come to appreciate the relationship between earth and food? Food and health? Food and peace? Land owners and field workers? Poor black farmers in the rural south and urbanized peasants in New Delhi? Mideast oil and farmers in Iowa?

Latin American sugar plantations and migrant farmworkers in Florida? The U.S. military budget and international grain reserves? Wendell Berry, in his book, *The Unsettling of America,* points to a basic forgetfulness upon which modern civilization is built: that is, the forgetfulness that the "civilized and the domestic continue to depend upon the wilderness, the natural forces within the climate and within the soil that have never in any meaningful sense been controlled or conquered." In the unfolding and spreading of industrial development, we have come to believe that "our dominion" does ultimately mean "our domination." Thus, through our mechanical creation, which greatly magnifies ourselves, we lose the ancient perception of the smallness of humanity within creation. We lose the awareness of our natural relationship to the Creator, to the earth, and to all that is within the earth. This spiritual distortion is reflected in the institutions and policies that rule our modern lives. It is interesting to note that how we treat the land is often a reflection of how we treat others—personally and corporately. Our forgetfulness of the mutuality that exists between the land, ourselves, and each other raises challenging questions in the contexts of democracy in America, the international community, and the people of the church: Who does own the land? What are policies and practices that affect land ownership patterns? How does the pattern of land ownership influence the quality of human life, particularly in rural areas, and how does it lead to the improvement or destruction of the health and productivity of the land itself?

The stewardship of land by God's people—his co-creators—is a central theme throughout the Old and New Testaments, as God reveals how his gifts to his people are to be used for the benefit of all. The modern perception of land as a market base, a primary source of political power, a tool of speculation, or a tax shelter is a far cry from the biblical concept of land as a God-given resource to be used for the health of the whole community.

In our urbanized society, many people are beginning to feel the pinch of disproportionate land ownership patterns as they are frustrated in their efforts to buy a home in a desirable market area, or as they are displaced from their homes by the buying and selling practices of land speculators. The struggle for control of the land and its fruits is, however, especially intense in the world's rural areas, as urbanization encroaches and populations grow. Worldwide, the absolute number of rural inhabitants continues to increase as population growth in many countries, 2.5–3.2 percent annually, surpasses urban migration. In most third world countries today, agriculture forms the basis of the economy. It is estimated that in these nations, from 50 to 90 percent of the population lives in rural areas. In the United States, rural populations are dwindling rapidly, while the nation's economy depends almost entirely on agriculture for its balance of payments: In 1978, the $48 billion trade deficit was reduced to $34 billion by the farm export surplus. Control of agricultural land is at the crux of problems now recognized as international priorities—malnutrition, rural–urban migration, burgeoning unemployment, soil erosion, and the continual denuding of the world's most important forests.

Land as Power

Land, especially good farmland, is a limited resource. In areas like the Ganges, Red, and Yangtze river basins, characterized by high population density and intensive agricultural production, land is scarce as compared to the abundant land available in areas like the many parts of Africa characterized by low population density and unintensive methods of farming. In most cases, the scarcity of land is not the result of unavoidable circumstances or natural conditions. It is brought about by patterns of land ownership that have been shaping human relations for hundreds of years. Land tenure is an important determinant of whether or not economic change will occur, what that change will be, and at what pace it will happen. Land is, in fact, the primary productive asset; knowing who holds the land tells us who holds economic and political power. In Africa, Asia, and Latin America, where three-fourths of the world's population lives, the control of farmland is the key to wealth, status, and power. Generally speaking, where a large share of the land is owned by a small proportion of the people, those people are the dominant forces in local politics; and as the lenders, the landlords, and the employers, they wield power in the economic lives of others. Even small- to medium-sized farms owned by a larger proportion of people offer a certain economic security and accompanying power; it is the landless and the near-landless who live on the economic bottom. Continually seeking work options to eke out a livelihood, they endure a survival existence totally dependent on the whims of those who do own the land. Many sell their labor to more fortunate farmers for whatever meager wages are available, or find employment on large estates or plantations as seasonal laborers. Others make arrangements with landlords for tenant farming or sharecropping. Most often these rental arrangements are at exorbitant rates under conditions so insecure as to eliminate any incentives for investment and technical progress. Still others try to get what they can be farming fragmented family plots and then seeking other employment to make ends meet. Women, often the hardest-working laborers, are among the most devastated by this situation; they have the least access to land rights.

These—the landless, the insecure tenants, those owning marginal plots—constitute the bulk of the "poorest of the poor," so often described by international development experts as the "targets" of aid policies that are designed to meet "basic human needs." Where is the meaning of land as power and the exploitation of the powerless by the powerful more pronounced than in war-torn Indochina? Once rich with fertile rice paddies, the land and its cultivators are victims of political violence and unimaginable destruction. With rare exceptions such as this one, the plight of the rural peasant is not recognized as a political one, which can be relieved only as the tools for living a whole life are redistributed to the poor. Just and enforceable land reform laws are a beginning. However, by themselves, these laws can be meaningless. The right of association and organization for the rural poor is essential, along with access to credit, improved seeds and tools, extension services, and a genuine political base.

As societies industrialize, new alternatives for power, such as non-agricultural jobs and new access to capital and modern technologies become available, and land ownership is no longer the sole source of one's livelihood. Yet our experience in the United States reminds us that land ownership remains a significant source of wealth and influence, even in the industrialized world. Only one in twenty-seven Americans live or work on farms, as compared to one in four in 1930. The narrowing of land ownership to a concentrated few raises much controversy about resource use, unemployment trends, and general community welfare.

Who Does Own The Land?

Worldwide statistics are staggering. They need not be adjusted to tell the story. A recent World Bank study indicates that in eighty-three countries just over 3 percent of the people own or control 80 percent of the agricultural land. This 3 percent represents the concentration of ownership of the vast majority of arable land in the hands of a minority of elites, often cooperating with each other.

In the United States, 70 percent of the population lives on less than 2 percent of the land. One of the most massive internal migrations in history has occurred in less than fifty years. Forty million people have streamed into metropolitan areas from the countryside. The amount of land in cultivation has increased while ownership has become more and more highly concentrated in fewer and fewer hands. Concurrently, agribusiness firms have expanded, and some 30,000 farms per year have been sold or abandoned, as the capital expenditures required for today's farming are beyond the reach of most families. Unfortunately, for those who do remain on the land, ownership does not necessarily mean control; frequently, farmers' choices regarding planting, cultivating, and harvesting are dictated by agribusiness concerns through advance sales contracts.

In the developing world there are endless examples of the inequitable distribution of land ownership. Eleven percent of Bangladesh's families own more than half of the country's land. In India, in 1971, 70 percent of the farms were smaller than two hectares (five acres) and included just 21 percent of the total farmland, while 4 percent of the farms were larger than ten hectares (twenty-five acres) and occupied 31 percent of the farmland. In the Philippines, in 1971, just 5 percent of the farms were larger than ten hectares, but they accounted for 34 percent of all cropland. Many families in the country have no land or employment at all. In 1975, the U.N. Food and Agricultural Organization (FAO) reported that in Latin America, where ownership is even more skewed, 7 percent of the landowners possessed a startling 93 percent of the arable land.

Land scarcity is emerging as a serious problem in many parts of sub-Saharan Africa. Poor soil and limited rainfall require extensive land use, populations are pressing against the arable land base, and traditional tribal-based tenure systems are giving way to more individual land rights, a development that leads to the accumulation of land by the wealthy and the accompanying absentee landlordism, tenancy, and landlessness. In Kenya, where colonial and independent governments have promoted this shift to private tenure, about 20 percent of rural households were landless in the early 1970s. The landless and near-landless constitute a majority of the rural land force in Asia and almost 80 percent in many Latin American countries.

Rapid Growth of the World's Landless and Near-Landless—Why?

The grossly disproportionate land ownership patterns are influenced by decisions of local and national governments as well as by foreign aid and investment policies. Both of these factors, and their relationship to each other, must be emphasized.

Local politics often promotes land accumulation by the more prosperous farmers, forced sales of land by marginal owners, and the eviction of tenants by landowners who want to profit from a new technique or input.

National policies determine farmers' rights to land, water, access to credit, transportation, and marketing. National governments control pricing, facilities for research, and the role that outside agents, such as AID (U.S. Agency for International Development) and private investors, will be allowed to play and how the benefits of such external influences will be distributed. Small farmers remain low on the list of most governments' priorities.

Nowhere can we find a more telling example than in the United States, where the lack of a unified national policy toward rural areas is at the core of the land tenure problem. The dramatic increase in the price of agricultural land—both the purchasing and rental price—is one of the major factors driving the small operator and the family farm out of business. Land is a very good investment, and the buying power of land speculators, corporations, and "hobby" farmers who use land ownership as a tax shelter has exerted a pressure most small farmers cannot withstand. The rate of land loss has been especially serious for Native Americans and black farmers in the South. Between 1950 and 1969, the white farm population was reduced by 45.3 percent, while in the same period, the minority population was reduced by 82.3 percent. Between 1964 and 1969, white farms decreased by 12.5 percent while black land ownership decreased by 37 percent. A large proportion of this loss has been due to legal maneuvers around the postbellum rural South policy of "heirs property," which allowed land to pass to a man's wife and children upon his death. The farmer-heir living and working on the land cannot secure full title to it without consent of all the other heirs, and the land has almost no market value. Yet, astute investors are able to persuade one of the heirs to sell them his or her interest in it, and they can then demand that their interest be partitioned from the rest of the tract. This often leads to a court order for the sale of the entire tract of land and a public auction in order to divide the proceeds among all heirs. Timber corporations, housing developers, and others are often among the bidders against whom the black farmer on heirs property must compete at the auction.

It is practices such as these that are chipping away at the viability of the American small family farm, and thus creating the need for a federal agricultural policy that would protect this country's farm families and create a self-sustaining, environmentally sound, economically stable food system for all of us.

How has the federal government moved so far from the Jeffersonian ideal of widespread ownership of independent family farms? The answer can be seen in the preference that large commercial farms have received in income and price support payments, which are based on volume and acreage, tax laws that involve undertaxation on capital gains from land and underassessment of large holdings, and publicly supported research and extension programs that benefit capital intensive farming.

In the absence of thoroughgoing land reform in many developing countries the extent and value of land holdings continue to determine the cultivators' access to credit. Without access to credit, the small farmer or landless peasant has no access to agricultural improvements, including fertilizer and tools. Sudhir Sen, an Indian economist and commentator on the Green Revolution, has estimated that roughly one-half of India's small farmers lack any recorded right to the land, without which they are unable to obtain crop loans from credit institutions. Additionally, small farmers are reluctant to use their land for loan collateral anyway—they don't want to risk losing their land. Small landholders, then, are dependent on private moneylenders and merchants known for their exorbitant rates of interest; and debt bondage is often used to tie peasants to the land to assure landowners that labor will be available. Sharecroppers who comprise a significant portion of the rural population in many developing countries are in a similar bind; they must provide all of the inputs in many cases, but they get only a portion of the crop. Obviously, they would need twice as great a prospect for advantage than owner-cultivators before being able to take a calculated risk for improvements. Insecure tenancy often results in soil depletion. The economic pressure on these tenants tells them that it would be unwise to take the usual protective measures of leaving fields fallow and rotating crops; such a judgment is not due to the alleged "backwardness" of the peasant farmer. The vicious cycle persists.

In most developing areas, development priorities have been biased toward the cities and mechanized high technology, even to the extent of widespread urban use of rural land. Little has been done to supply the marginalized farmer with alternative employment opportunities in the rural areas. As a result, the landless are pushed toward and pulled in by the promise of urban areas. They are not prepared to meet the prevailing problems of rising unemployment, overcrowded slums, and cultural disintegration. This reality is heightened by startling demographic pressures in rural areas. Many rural populations are still growing at 2 percent or more per year, yielding a doubling within thirty-five years.

Just as is true in industry, capital intensive growth in the agricultural sector has led to the deterioration of the income of the poor. The emphasis on growing cash crops, often the traditional plantation crops, which are demanded by the urban elites in their own country and abroad and supplied by the rural poor, demonstrates the small farmers' lack of influence in the marketplace—nationally and internationally.

This leads us to the very important role of the international market in determining how land is used. The international market is tightly controlled by industrial countries' trading policies and the activities of multinational corporations. From the sixteenth to the nineteenth century, Africa, Asia, Latin America, and the Caribbean were integrated into the economic system of Europe through colonialism. Their economies were oriented to provide both natural resources for use in European industry and agricultural products for consumption by European populations. To a large extent this imbalance in growth persists today, as third world countries concentrate on agricultural and resource production for export, while manufacturing and industry is monopolized by corporations in Europe, North America, and Japan. This means that independence for most third world countries has not brought significant change in the economic system established by colonial powers. It is the local elites, once nurtured by the colonial powers, now wealthy in land, who invite foreign investment and ownership. For example, the recent Nicaraguan revolution was a direct uprising against one of the most oppressive export cropping systems in Latin America, shored up by Somoza's repressive government. Among other things, the ruling family and their friends controlled the production and export of coffee and expanded their beef, cotton, and sugar operations at the expense of nearly every sector of the population, particularly rural peasants.

In his book, *Persistent Poverty,* George Beckford points to the economies most controlled by plantation enterprises:

> British enterprises account for the bulk of West Indian sugar production and trade; United States enterprises, for the bulk of sugar output and trade in Puerto Rico, the Dominican Republic, Haiti, and the Philippines; U.S. rubber companies, for almost all of the total rubber output in Liberia; U.S. companies, for close to the total banana output and trade of the Central American republics; Australian companies, for all of the raw sugar in Fiji; and American, British, Dutch, and other European companies, for most of the rubber, tea, and oil palm and for the trade in Ceylon and Southeast Asia.

In the Philippines, one-third of the arable land is devoted to export crops, largely bananas, copra, coconuts, and pineapples grown on plantations. The big landlords of fifty hectares or more are no longer found in the rice and corn lands, but rather in plantation lands exempt from land reform laws. The end result, as in many cases, is a tremendous decline in the production of food for local consumption—often the staple crops or the foods richest in protein, necessary for the maintenance of the health and nutritional status of those who do not benefit from the cash cropping. This situation is recognized as one of the most important factors behind the high mortality rate among children of the most vulnerable ages, zero to five years, which in the Philippines exceeds 50 percent.

In Sri Lanka, 150 years after the British plantation entrepreneurs established the tea estates, the plantations dominate the hill countryside and the economy of the whole country. In 1961, 180 pounds of tea could buy one ton of rice in the world market, but in 1974, Sri Lanka required 684 pounds of tea for the same ton of rice.

The beef market in Costa Rica provides another vivid demonstration of the problems invoked by export cropping, apart from problems of the traditional plantation economies described above. The United States is the world's largest importer of beef, and historically beef imports have been used as protection against rising beef prices in this country. Since demand began to rise rapidly in the late 1950s, the contributions of USAID, the World Bank, the Inter-American Development Bank, and private investment soared in the beef-exporting countries of Guatemala, Nicaragua, Costa Rica, Haiti, Honduras, Mexico, Argentina, and El Salvador. While total imports from Costa

Rica have risen dramatically and large ranchers have benefited greatly, the impact on the average Costa Rican has been very damaging. With the influx of foreign capital, the beef industry is now expanded to the point of occupying more than 50 percent of Costa Rica's total land area. Much of that is land that was once used by small family farmers to grow basic foodstuffs and supply their own needs. The livestock industry monopolizes 60 percent of the financial credit destined for agriculture, while displaced farmers have fled to cities only to find unemployment instead of work. While average annual beef consumption in the United States rose from 80 to 112 pounds between 1955 and 1973, the average Costa Rican experienced a decline in beef consumption from 48 pounds per year to a meal of meat about five times per year. There is, in essence, a competition between United States and Costa Rican consumers.

The United States imports nearly $10 billion worth of agricultural products from poor countries where malnutrition and hunger are rampant. It is our essential responsibility to recognize the linkages between U.S. investment, the American farmer, and the American consumer and the plight of the displaced in countries such as Costa Rica. This web of cause and effect is brought very close to home when we ask, "what about the onslaught of illegal aliens from Mexico in our southwest?"

In summary, then, it is no wonder that the three reasons most often put forth to explain the lack of capability of countries to feed their own masses are: (1) inadequate government policy regarding land ownership; (2) foreign investment and inappropriate investment of the elites in their own nations; and (3) political instability.

But What about National Growth and Productivity?

Unjust land ownership patterns have obvious social and economic consequences for the marginal and landless peasant, but what about the consequences for national growth? What about the trickle-down effect? In actuality, growth in a nation's gross national product is no longer accepted as an adequate indicator of the benefits of agricultural or industrial development. As national planners and development theorists have become more aware of the widening gap between rich and poor, they have shifted their priorities toward a strategy of redistribution with growth—a balanced emphasis on productivity and equity.

What about productivity? Haven't big farmers proved to be more efficient and resourceful than small ones? The argument usually goes something like this: Big farmers are more willing to take risks. They have become big and stayed big because they have the intelligence, the capital, and the management talent; and they can, therefore, afford the mechanization that leads to increased efficiency. Interestingly enough, evidence is accumulating to show that small-scale farms can be highly productive and can, in fact, outproduce large farms on a per-acre basis. Equity and efficiency are not necessarily at odds. FAO data comparing per-hectare output on farms smaller than five hectares with per-hectare output on farms larger than twenty hectares reveal higher gross productivity on the smaller units in many countries. In India, for example, production on the smaller units average 80 percent more than on larger farms. On the other hand, when large modernized export crop plantations are compared with peasant farms in Jamaica or Peru, the big units show far higher putput. Such comparisons do not allow for differences in climate, soils, and crop type, nor for the advantages of larger farmers in terms of credit and inputs. Among the many factors affecting productivity other than size, the Land Tenure Center has found that the most important factor is the relationship of the people to the land. Small farms can be very productive, as in Japan, where people working on them know that the productivity will benefit them. Likewise, productivity on large farms can excell if the people working the land are assured that the fruits of their labor will benefit them. This is not the case in the large farms of the Soviet Union, nor is it true on many large farms in the United States and developing countries where absenteeism and pure profit motivation characterizes the large landholders. Workers are not directly benefited by their labor, nor are the growers directly responsible for the health of the land. In Mexico, in the early 1960s large commercial growers found that they could increase their profits enormously without even trying to increase their yields. They simply expanded their holdings and received subsidies from the government. Additionally, it has been revealed that much of the profit of large commercial farms goes toward the consumption of luxury items by the elite, rather than being channeled back into new agricultural input. Furthermore, the literal waste of valuable land by large landholding interests, especially plantations, is astounding. A study discussed by Lappe and Collins in their book, *Food First,* revealed that farmers who own up to ten acres cultivate 72 percent of their land, but farmers with over eighty-six acres cultivate only 14 percent of their land. They use 49 percent for pasture, and leave 37 percent idle (FAO, "Agricultural Development and Employment Performance: A Comparative Analysis," *Agricultural Planning Studies,* no. 18, 1974, p. 124). If large landowners are the most wasteful of the land, could they be counted on as the best hope for agricultural development? In summary, smaller farms tend to outproduce large farms, mainly because of the greater labor inputs and personal attention they receive.

The evidence does not support the notion that large-scale commercial farms are more efficient, nor does it demonstrate the alleged advantages of increasingly interdependent world food trade for local populations. What, then, are the justifications for uncontrolled corporate growth in agriculture? Current realities tell us that we have been willing to replace regional self-sufficiency as a primary goal of agriculture with a blind trust in the unlimited control of our food-producing resources by a minority of large landowners. Are there, in fact, any positive effects of the growing dependence of more and more people on fewer and fewer producers for their food? Undoubtedly, profits for the local large landholders and corporate growers skyrocket. The ultimate benefits of these profits on a nation's overall economy is debatable, as are the ultimate benefits of a "beefed-up" gross national product for the most needy in a nation. Undoubtedly, there is more variety on more dinner tables of consumers in urban areas and in industrial nations as a whole—and at lower costs. How committed are we to such benefits?

When viewed from the perspective of the quality of life as experienced by the majority of people at all points in the land ownership–land use–food production–food distribution–nutrition cycle, the conclusion we reach is clear. The linkages among the existing patterns of land ownership, our lives, and the lives of the rural poor are easily identified. Increased concentration of land in the hands of a few necessarily means the marginalization of a growing number of people and a growing number of acres of arable land. Land is a unique and limited resource—the center of the agrarian society that provides our sustenance; and the quality of life of those eliminated from their rights to this resource is severely threatened. Increased access to land and its benefits necessarily means improved health, education, and the general well-being of rural people. In the words of George Beckman, "social welfare does not mean only material welfare. Material advancement can be satisfactory only if it preserves the quality of life that people themselves regard as important (*Persistent Poverty,* "Preface")." In his view, this means genuine independence—the full freedom of a people to control the environment in which they live.

In our own country, the urban-oriented society does not usually recognize that 40 percent of the nation's poor lives in nonmetropolitan areas, that 34 percent of the total population lives in nonmetropolitan areas, and that federal poverty relief programs fail to reflect the disproportionate level of rural poverty. On a worldwide scale, 61 percent of the world's population lives in rural areas. Six hundred million live in rural households that are landless or lack secure access to adequate farmland—a fact that should stir us to the core of our commitment to the divine provider of bread and justice for all people.

As consumers, as landowners, as policy-makers, as followers of Jesus, is there no way we can express our insistence that all people enjoy this unique and permanent gift of our Creator? Is there no way we can express our outrage with the present realities that victimize those who are poor? It is time to see the just distribution of land as the beginning of a new remembrance of our individual and corporate relationship to the life of the land.

SELECTION A
ABUNDANT REWARD OF RECLAIMING A MARGINAL FARM

by Wendell Berry *
Reprinted from *Smithsonian,* August, 1980.

One day in the summer of 1956, leaving home for school, I stopped on the side of the road directly above the house where I now live. From there you could see a mile or so across the Kentucky River Valley, and perhaps six miles along the length of it. The valley was a green trough full of sunlight, blue in its distances. I often stopped here in my comings and goings, just to look, for it was all familiar to me from before the time my memory began: woodlands and pastures on the hillsides; fields and croplands, wooded slough-edges and hollows in the bottoms; and through the midst of it the treelined

*NOTE: *Wendell Berry is a poet, teacher and proponent of small-scale farming. His most recent book is* **A Part,** *which includes poems about his farm.*

river passing down from its headwaters near the Virginia line toward its mouth at Carrollton on the Ohio.

Standing there, I was looking at land where one of my great-great-great-grandfathers settled in 1803, and at the scene of some of the happiest times of my own life, where in my growing-up years I camped, hunted, fished, boated, swam and wandered—where, in short, I did whatever escaping I felt called upon to do. It was a place where I had happily been, and where I always wanted to be. And I remember gesturing toward the valley that day and saying to the friend who was with me: "That's all I need."

I meant it. It was an honest enough response to my recognition of its beauty, the abundance of its lives and possibilities, and of my own love for it and interest in it. And in the sense that I continue to recognize all that, and feel that what I most need is here, I can still say the same thing.

And yet I am aware that I must necessarily mean something different—or at least a great deal more—when I say it now. Then I was speaking mostly from affection, and did not know, by half, what I was talking about. I was speaking of a place that in some ways I knew and in some ways cared for, but did not live in. The differences between knowing a place and living in it, between cherishing a place and living responsibly in it, had not begun to occur to me. But they are critical differences, and understanding them has been the chief necessity of my experience since then.

I married in the following summer, and in the next seven years lived in a number of distant places. But, largely because I continued to feel that what I needed was here, I could never bring myself to want to live in any other place. And so we returned to live in Kentucky in the summer of 1964, and that autumn bought the house whose roof my friend and I had looked down on eight years before, and with it "twelve acres more or less." Thus began a profound change in my life. Before, I had lived according to expectation rooted in ambition. Now I began to live according to a kind of destiny rooted in my origins and in my life. One should not speak too confidently of one's "destiny"; I use the word to refer to causes that lie deeper in history and character than mere intention or desire. In buying the little place known as Lanes Landing, it now seems to me, I began to obey these deeper causes.

We had returned so that I could take a job at the University of Kentucky in Lexington. And we expected to live pretty much the usual academic life: I would teach and write; my "subject matter" would be, as it had been, the few square miles in Henry Country where I grew up. We bought the tiny farm at Lanes Landing, thinking that we would use it as a "summer place," and on that understanding I began, with the help of two carpenter friends, to make some necessary repairs on the house. I no longer remember exactly how it was decided, but that work had hardly begun when it became a full-scale overhaul. By so little our minds had been changed: this was not going to be a house to visit, but a house to live in. It was as though, having put our hand to the plow, we not only did not look back, but could not. We renewed the old house, equipped it with plumbing, bathroom and oil furnace, and moved in on July 4, 1965.

Once the house was whole again, we came under the influence of the "twelve-acres more or less." This acreage included a steep hillside pasture, two small pastures by the river, and a "garden spot" of less than half an acre. We had, besides the house, a small barn in bad shape, a good large building that once had been a general store, and a small garage also in usable condition. This was hardly a farm by modern standards, but it was land that could be used, and it was unthinkable that we would not use it. The land was not good enough to afford the possibility of a cash income, but it would allow us to grow our food—or most of it. And that is what we set out to do.

In the early spring of 1965 I had planted a small orchard; the next spring we planted our first garden. Within the following six or seven years we reclaimed the pastures, converted the garage into a henhouse, rebuilt the barn, greatly improved the garden soil, planted berry bushes, acquired a milk cow—and were producing, except for hay and grain for our animals, nearly everything that we ate: fruit, vegetables, eggs, meat, milk, cream and butter. We built an outbuilding with a meat room and a food-storage cellar. Because we did not want to pollute our land and water with sewage, and in the process waste nutrients that should be returned to the soil, we build a composting privy. And so we began to attempt a life that, in addition to whatever else it was, would be responsibly agricultural. We used no chemical fertilizers. Except for a little rotenone, we used no insecticides. As our land and our food became healthier, so did we.

We were not, of course, living an idyll. What we had done could not have been accomplished without difficulty and a great deal of work. And we had made some mistakes and false starts. But there was great satisfaction, too, in restoring the neglected land, and in feeding ourselves from it.

Meanwhile, the 40-acre place adjoining ours on the downriver side had been sold to a "developer," who planned to divide it into 114 lots for "second homes." This project was probably doomed by the steepness of the ground and the difficulty of access, but a lot of bulldozing—and a lot of damage—was done before it was given up. In the fall of 1972, the place was offered for sale and we were able to buy it.

We now began to deal with larger agricultural problems. Some of this new land was usable; some would have to be left in trees. There were perhaps 15 acres of hillside that could be reclaimed for pasture, and about two-and-a-half acres of excellent bottomland on which we would grow alfalfa for hay. But it was a mess, all of it badly neglected, and a considerable portion of it badly abused by the developer's bulldozers. The hillsides were covered with thicket growth; the bottom was shoulder high in weeds; the diversion ditches had to be restored; a bulldozed gash meant for "building sites" had to be mended; the barn needed a new foundation, and the cistern a new top; there were no fences. What we had bought was less a farm than a reclamation project—which has now, with a later purchase, grown to 75 acres.

While we had only the small place, I had got along very well with a Gravely "walking tractor" that I owned, and an old Farmall A that I occasionally borrowed from my Uncle Jimmy. But now that we had increased our acreage, it was clear that I could not continue to depend on a borrowed tractor. For a while I assumed that I would buy a tractor of my own. But because our land was steep, and there was already talk of a fuel shortage—and because I liked the idea—I finally decided to buy a team of horses instead. By the spring of 1973, after a lot of inquiring and looking, I had found and bought a team of five-year-old sorrel mares. And—again by the generosity of my Uncle Jimmy, who has never thrown any good thing away—I had enough equipment to make a start.

Farming as It Was Done in My Boyhood

Though I had worked horses and mules during the time I was growing up, I had never worked over ground so steep and problematical as this, and it had been 20 years since I had worked a team over ground of any kind. Getting started again, I anticipated every new task with uneasiness, and sometimes with dread. But to my relief and delight, the team and I did all that needed to be done that year, getting better as we went along. And over the years since then, with that team and others, my son and I have carried on our farming the way it was carried on in my boyhood, doing everything with our horses except baling the hay. And we have done work in places and in weather in which a tractor would have been useless. Experience has shown us—or reshown us— that horses are not only a satisfactory and economical means of power, especially on such small places as ours, but are probably *necessary* to the most conservative use of steep land. Our farm, in fact, is surrounded by potentially excellent hillsides that were maintained in pasture until tractors replaced the teams.

Another change in our economy (and our lives) was accomplished in the fall of 1973 with the purchase of our first wood-burning stove. Again the petroleum shortage was on our minds, but we also knew that from the pasture-clearing we had ahead of us we would have an abundance of wood that otherwise would go to waste—and when that was gone we would still have our permanent woodlots. We thus expanded our subsistence income to include heating fuel, and since then have used our furnace only as a "backup system" in the coldest weather and in our absences from home. The horses also contribute significantly to the work of fuel-gathering; they will go easily into difficult places and over soft ground or snow where a truck or a tractor could not move.

As we have continued to live on and from our place, we have slowly begun its restoration and healing. Most of the scars have now been mended and grassed over, most of the washes stopped, most of the buildings made sound; many loads of rocks have been hauled out of the fields and used to pave entrances or fill hollows; we have done perhaps half of the necessary fencing. A great deal of work is still left to do, and some of it—the rebuilding of fertility in the depleted hillsides—will take longer than we will live. But in doing these things we have begun a restoration and a healing in ourselves.

I should say plainly that this has not been a "paying proposition." As a reclamation project, it has been costly both in money and in effort. It seems at least possible that, in any other place, I might have had little interest in doing any such thing. The reason I have been interested in doing it here, I think, is that I have felt implicated in the history, the uses and the attitudes that have depleted such places as ours and made them "marginal."

I had not worked long on our "twelve acres more or less" before I saw that such places were explained almost as much by their human history as by their nature. I saw that they were not "marginal" because they ever were unfit for human use, but because in both culture and character *we* had been unfit to use them. Originally, even such steep slopes as these along the lower Kentucky River Valley were deep-soiled and abundantly fertile; "jumper" plows and generations of carelessness impoverished them. Where yellow clay is at the surface now, five feet of good soil may be gone. I once wrote that on some of the nearby uplands one walks as if "knee-deep" in the absence of the original soil. On these steeper slopes, I now know, that absence is shoulder-deep.

That is a loss that is horrifying as soon as it is imagined. It happened easily, by ignorance, indifference, "a little folding of the hands to sleep." It cannot be remedied in human time; to build five feet of soil takes perhaps 50,000 years. This loss, once imagined, is potent with despair. If a people, in adding 150 years to itself, subtracts 50,000 years from its land, what is there to hope?

And so our reclamation project has been, for me, less a matter of idealism or morality than a kind of self-preservation. A destructive history, once it is understood as such, is a nearly insupportable burden. Understanding it is a disease of understanding, depleting the sense of efficacy and paralyzing effort, unless it finds healing work. For me that work has been partly of the mind, in what I have written, but that seems to have depended inescapably on work of the body and of the ground. In order to affirm the values most native and necessary to me—indeed, to affirm my own life as a thing decent in possibility—I needed to know in my own experience that this place did not have to be abused in the past, and that it can be kindly and conservingly used now.

With certain reservations that must be strictly borne in mind, our work here seems to have begun to offer some of the needed proofs.

Bountiful as the vanished original soil of the hillsides may have been, what remains is good. It responds well—sometimes astonishingly well—to good treatment. It never should have been plowed (some of it never should have been cleared), and it never should be plowed again. But it can be put in pasture without plowing, and it will support an excellent grass sod that will in turn protect it from erosion, if properly managed and not overgrazed.

Land so steep as this will not support a commercial, broken-field agriculture. To subject it to such an expectation is simply to ruin it, as its history shows. Our rule, generally has been to plow no steep ground, to maintain in pasture only such clopes as can be safely mowed with a horse-drawn mower, and to leave the rest in trees. We have increased the numbers of livestock on our pastures gradually, and have carefully rotated the animals from field to field, in order to avoid overgrazing. Under this use and care, our hillsides have mended and they produce more and better pasturage every year.

As a child, I always intended to be a farmer. As a young man, I gave up that intention, assuming that I could not farm and do the other things I wanted to do. And then I became a farmer almost unintentionally and by a kind of necessity. That wayward and necessary becoming—along with my marriage, which has been intimately a part of it—is the major event of my life. It has changed me profoundly from the man and the writer I would otherwise have been.

There was a time, after I had left home and before I came back, when this place was my "subject matter." I meant that too, I think, on the day in 1956 when I told my friend, "That's all I need." I was regarding it, in a way too easy for a writer, as a mirror in which I saw myself. There was obviously a sort of narcissism in that—and an inevitable superficiality, for only the surface can reflect.

In coming home and settling on this place, I began to *live* in my subject, and to learn that living in one's subject is not at all the same as "having" a subject. One's relation to one's subject ceases to be merely emotional or esthetical, or even merely critical, and becomes problematical, practical and responsible as well. Because it must. It is like marrying your sweetheart.

A Small income from "Unfarmable" Land

Though our farm has not been an economic success, as such success is usually reckoned, it is nevertheless beginning to make a kind of economic sense that is consoling and hopeful. Now that the largest expenses of purchase and repair are behind us, our income from the place is beginning to run ahead of expenses. As income I am counting the value of shelter, subsistence, heating fuel, and money earned by the sale of livestock. As expenses I am counting maintenance, newly purchased equipment, extra livestock feed, newly purchased animals, reclamation work, fencing materials, taxes and insurance.

If our land had been in better shape when we bought it, our expenses would obviously be much smaller. As it is, once we have completed its restoration, our farm will provide us a home, produce our subsistence, keep us warm in winter, and earn a modest cash income. The significance of this becomes apparent when one considers that most of this land is "unfarmable" by the standards of conventional agriculture, and that most of it was producing nothing at the time we bought it.

And so, contrary to some people's opinion, it *is* possible for a family to live on such "marginal" land, to take a bountiful subsistence and some cash income from it, and, in doing so, to improve both the land and themselves. (I believe however that, at least in the present economy, this should not be attempted without a source of income other than the farm. It is now extremely difficult to pay for the best of farmland by farming it, and even "marginal" land has become unreasonably expensive. To attempt to make a living from such land is to impose a severe strain on land and people alike.)

I said earlier that the success of our work here is subject to reservations. The first is that land like ours—and there are many acres of such land in this country—can be conserved in use only by competent knowledge, by a great deal more work than is required by leveler land, by a devotion more particular and disciplined than patriotism, and by ceaseless watchfulness and care. All these are cultural values and resources, never abundant in this country, and now almost obliterated by the contrary values of the "affluent society."

One of my own mistakes will suggest the difficulty. In 1974 I dug a small pond on a wooded hillside that I wanted to pasture occasionally. The excavation for that pond—as I should have anticipated, for I had better reason than I used—caused the hillside to slump both above and below. After six years the slope has not stabilized, and more expense and trouble will be required. A small hillside farm will not survive many mistakes of that order. Nor will a modest income.

The true remedy for such mistakes is to keep from making them. It is not the piecemeal technological solution that our society now offers, but a change of cultural (and economic) values that will encourage in the whole population the necessary respect, restraint and care. Even more important, it is the possibility of settled families and local communities, in which the knowledge of proper means and methods, proper moderations and restraints, can be handed down, and so accumulate in place and stay alive; the experience of one generation is not adequate to inform and control its actions. Such possibilities are not now in sight.

The second reservation is that we live at the lower end of a watershed that has long been intensively used, and is increasingly abused. Strip mining, logging, extractive farming, and the digging, draining, roofing and paving that go with industrial and urban "development," all have seriously depleted the capacity of the watershed to retain water. This means not only that floods are higher and more frequent than they would be if the watershed were healthy, but that the floods subside too quickly, the watershed being far less a sponge, now, than it is a roof. The floodwater drops suddenly out of the river, leaving the steep banks soggy, heavy and soft. As a result, great strips and blocks of land crack loose and slump, or they give way entirely and disappear into the river in what people here call "slips."

The flood of December 1978, which was unusually high, also went down extremely fast, falling from bank top almost to pool stage within a couple of days. In the aftermath of this rapid "drawdown," we lost a block of bottomland an acre square. This slip, which is still crumbling, severely damaged our place, and may eventually undermine two buildings. The same flood started a slip in another place, which threatens a third building. We have yet another building situated on a huge (but, so far, very gradual) slide that starts at the river and, aggravated by two state highway cuts, goes almost to the hilltop. And we have serious riverbank erosion the whole length of our place.

What this means is that, no matter how successfully we may control erosion on our hillsides, our land remains susceptible to a more serious cause of erosion that we cannot control. Our riverbanks stand literally at the cutting edge of our nation's consumptive economy. This, I think, is true of many "marginal" places—is true, in fact, of many places that are not marginal. In its consciousness, ours is an upland society; the ruin of watersheds, and what that involves and means, is little considered. And so the land is heavily taxed to subsidize an "affluence" that consists, in reality, of health and goods stolen from the unborn.

Living at the lower end of the Kentucky River watershed is what is now known as "an educational experience"—and not an easy one. A lot of information comes with it that is severely damaging to the reputation of our people and our time. From where I live and work, I never have to look far to see that the earth does indeed pass away. But however that is taught, and however bitterly learned, it is something that should be known, and there is a certain good strength in knowing it. To spend one's life farming a piece of the earth so passing is, as many would say, a hard lot. But it is, in an ancient sense, the human lot. What saves it is to love the farming.

SELECTION B
THE DESTRUCTION OF BLACK WOLF
by Denise Giardina
Reprinted from *Sojourners,* November, 1979.

In 1960, Black Wolf, West Virginia, was a tiny coal-mining town of 48 people with a store, community garden, and playground. In 1979, one house stands at Black Wolf, surrounded by the crumbling foundations of the others. The playground, the garden, the sagging fences which once marked off yards are covered with tangles of weeds and briars.

The destruction of Black Wolf was brought about by economic forces which have oppressed and systematically pillaged an entire region of this nation: the coal-mining areas of the central Appalachian mountains.

The people of Black Wolf, employees of Crozier Coal Company, did not own their homes or the land they lived on. Their houses were the property of Crozier Coal. The land was and is owned by the Pocahontas Land Company, a subsidiary of Norfolk and Western Railroad and the Consolidation Coal Company, a division of Continental Oil. These companies leased Black Wolf to a succession of coal companies for the purpose of mining coal and maintaining employees on the land.

In the late 1950s and early 1960s, the coal industry slumped drastically. The miners bore the brunt of economic disaster. Mines around Black Wolf closed or were cut back and a mass exodus began. In southern Virginia alone, between 1960 and 1970, more than 176,000 people left, nearly 25 per cent of the population. McDowell County, in which Black Wolf is located, lost almost half of its 90,000 people between 1950 and 1970.

Many who left traded family and roots for a precarious existence in the slums of northern cities. Others who stayed found themselves on welfare and on the television news as Lyndon Johnson's "War on Poverty" focused on the mountains of Appalachia.

The people of Black Wolf also left to find jobs, and one by one their houses were torn down by the coal company. Finally, only one family remained, George and Susie Lovett and their four children. George Lovett was one of hundreds of miners who stayed on the company payroll and worked only when called. Three days of work was a very good week, one or two days was more common; often the mine stayed closed. Miners were only paid for the days they worked. And so George Lovett worked sporadically at one of the most dangerous jobs in the world, while his family wore donated, patched clothes and ate pinto beans nearly every night in their four-room house.

The 1970s brought change as the energy crisis renewed demand for Appalachian coal. Mines reopened, work became steady, and homesick people began to move back to the coalfields. George Lovett was able to work full time and provide for his family. Then in 1971 he fell onto a conveyor belt in the mine and was crushed to death. The Lovett family was forced to leave Black Wolf soon after, and their house too was torn down.

The story of Black Wolf and the Lovett family could be retold throughout the Appalachian coalfields with only a change in name. The renewed interest in coal has meant work and decent wages for those in mining occupations and fortunes for the energy corporations. It has also meant a continued deterioration in the quality of life in the coalfields. McDowell County business boosters boast of being in the "Heart of the Billion Dollar Coalfield." Few of those billion dollars have gone to benefit the people of McDowell County and the rest of southern West Virginia. Consider the following:

- Coal mining continues to lead the nation's industry in accidents and fatalities. Since 1906, 92,000 coal miners have been killed and at least 1,660,000 have been injured or disabled. In 1977, 142 United States miners died. In 1969, more than 100,000 miners were judged by the Public Health Service to be afflicted with black lung, or pneumoconiosis. Black lung occurs as coal dust is breathed into the lungs, and its effects can be anything from shortening of breath to death.

- Strip mining continues to cause tremendous environmental damage. The sides and tops of mountains have been removed, marring the landscape and sending mud and rockslides onto houses below. Army Corps of Engineers' records show a fourfold increase over a period of 20 years in floods along the Tug River, which originates in heavily stripped McDowell County.

  A 1977 flood left 1,372 families homeless in McDowell and Mingo Counties and caused millions of dollars in damage.

  Deep mining has also harmed the environment. A drive anywhere in McDowell County will show massive "slag heaps" or "gob piles" pouring down the sides of mountains. These are large, black piles of the waste from processed coal. Many slag heaps are almost as large as the mountains they cover. It was such a slag heap which burst in 1972 on Buffalo Creek in Logan County, sending a wall of water into the hollow which killed 125 people and destroyed many homes.

  Deep mines have also polluted streams, which 50 years ago were full of fish, by allowing acid to run into the water.

- Most of McDowell County does not have access to sewage treatment plants or garbage service. Most sewer lines up and down the hollows run directly into creeks. Garbage which has piled up also finds its way into the streams. The branches of bushes along the creek beds are decorated with bits of toilet paper, tin cans, and plastic bleach bottles.

- The quality of medical care is well below the nation's as a whole. In McDowell County there is only one general practitioner for every 8,000 people.

  In central Appalachia (southern West Virginia, eastern Kentucky, and southwest Virginia) 25 per cent of the population has no medical insurance. Poor people in waiting rooms report being passed over in favor of paying patients, and often wait all day without seeing a doctor. Infant and maternal mortality rates are much higher than the national average.

- Monthly incomes of $140 to $225 are common in mineral-rich McDowell. For those who cannot find employment with a coal company, job possibilities are nearly non-existent.
- In central Appalachia, 37 per cent of all housing is without complete plumbing and 40 per cent of all housing is rated as substandard. In most of the hollows of McDowell County, no new housing has been built in 40 years, although hundreds of houses have been torn down.
- The influx of people back into the area seeking employment has put a tremendous pressure on the whole region. A recent government survey predicted that the next 20 years would see everything from skyrocketing crime rates to outbreaks of sanitation-related epidemics.

Anyone attempting to address any of these problems quickly runs head-on into the biggest obstacle of all, the root cause of the oppression of McDowell County—land ownership.

There are 344,576 acres of land in McDowell County. Six corporations own 246,943 acres, and in all, around 85 per cent of the land is corporate-owned. By far the largest landowner is the Pocahontas Land Company, a subsidiary of the Norfolk and Western Railroad, which owns 110,887 acres, or nearly one-third of McDowell County, including Black Wolf. Other large landowners in McDowell County include Georgia-Pacific and Consolidation Coal Company (Continental Oil), with 68,000 acres between them.

Corporate land is appraised at an unbelievably low price, much of it at less than $40 an acre. The resulting low property taxes of approximately 50 cents an acre allow companies to hold on to undeveloped land and deprive local government of needed income.

When an offer is made to buy corporate land, the value suddenly jumps. In neighboring Mingo County, the state of West Virginia attempted to purchase land owned by the Cotiga Development Company of Philadelphia in order to build new housing for flood victims. The land, valued at $36 an acre for tax purposes, was offered to the state for $4,000 an acre. But in most cases, the corporations refuse to consider selling.

The land of central Appalachia has been in the hands of the corporations for almost a century. It was taken from people isolated from the outside world by their mountains, people for whom the value system of a newly industrialized America was alien. Methods varied from legal trickery to fraud to the sheer weight of dollars. My own great-grandparents sold an entire coal-rich hollow in Kentucky for $50, a sum they had never seen in their lives. For the shrewdest mountaineers, who refused to sell, violence could be a very convincing means of persuasion.

In some cases, the corporations bought the minerals beneath the land, while leaving mountain people in possession of the surface of the land. Those people who sold their ''mineral rights'' had no idea what the implications would be. It is their children and grandchildren who have paid the price, as they have been evicted from homes and seen the land they own torn apart as corporations dig ''their'' minerals. To date, courts have always ruled that mineral rights take precedence over surface rights.

However, most people in the coalfields do not own even the surface rights, although many now own their houses. But if a corporation decides it wants its land, ownership of a home means nothing. In 1976, the 32 families of Hutchinson, West Virginia, including homeowners, were evicted by the Pittston Company, which wanted to build a coal processing plant on the site. The houses were all bulldozed, and Hutchinson no longer exists.

Nothing will change in southern West Virginia as long as the corporations own the land. They have succeeded not only in gaining economic and political control of the region, they have also destroyed the fabric of life of a unqiue area of this country. People with strong ties to family and to the land have been uprooted, shoved together into poor housing, forced to work for the one industry which has caused all the destruction.

In the midst of such a situation, God has pronounced the liberating word: jubilee. ''In this year of jubilee you shall return, every one of you to his patrimony. When you sell or buy land amongst yourselves, neither party shall drive a hard bargain. If a man cannot afford to buy back the property, it shall remain in the hands of the purchaser till the year of jubilee. It shall then revert to the original owner'' (Leviticus 25:13–14, 28).

Jesus made clear that his coming was the sign of the proclamation of jubilee, the ''acceptable year of the Lord'' which the prophet Isaiah had spoken of. Certainly jubilee has not been fully realized, and will not be until God acts. But Jesus' life and words demonstrate the reality of jubilee for us now.

The poor of McDowell County are strong in their religious faith. They speak freely about the suffering of Jesus which surpassed their own suffering, about the sinfulness of greed and wealth, about love and family as life's most important gifts. They have no doubt that they will someday have their reward. They are the heirs of the kingdom. But they are just as sure that only when they are dead will they know justice. The church has failed to bring the liberating word of jubilee into the present and has kept from the poor of the coalfields the joyful knowledge of God's mighty work now.

In the meantime, Black Wolf stands empty, like scores of other ghost towns throughout the mountains. It could provide housing, a place to raise children who run freely and climb mountains, a place to build a new community. Instead, it lies beneath its weeds and groans with the rest of creation. straining to see the day when the children of God come into their own.

Session 5

HOLDING UP HALF THE SKY

Bible Study and Discussion

Luke 1:46–55
I Samuel 2:1–10
Revelation 12:1–6, 13–17

- Read and discuss the three Scriptural passages.
- What do these Biblical passages suggest about the place of women within salvation history?
- What vision has the writer of Revelation concerning the birth pangs of a new life?

Moving Along

- In the essay, "Holding Up Half the Sky" (pp. 60–65), two questions are asked: What can women do for rural development, and what can development do for women? What answers are suggested to you by the essay?
- Referring back to your discussion in Session 3, page 19, on "structures" for development, did you include the role of women?
- In Selection A, pages 65–66, concerning the World Conference of the United Nations Decade for Women, there is mention of a "self-reliant program." If you were designing this program, what would you include?
- If you were asked to conduct a program for your congregation around the topic, "The New Role of Women in Third World Development," what would you include in that program?
- What does the term "holding up half the sky" mean to you?

Preparing for the Next Session

- Identify a moderator for the next session.

• Ask the participants to write a prayer or litany concerning the role of women in development for the next session.

Ending

• Read aloud:
  Genesis 18:1, 9–15; 21:1–6
• Pause for silent meditation and reflection.
• Read together:
  Psalm 113
• Share the prayers of the participants.
• Read aloud:

A Prayer attributed to St. Francis

> Lord, make us instruments of your peace. Where there is hatred, let us sow love; where there is injury, pardon; where there is discord, union; where there is doubt, faith; where there is despair, hope; where there is darkness, light; where there is sadness, joy. Grant that we may not so much seek to be consoled as to console; to be understood as to understand; to be loved as to love. For it is in giving that we receive; it is in pardoning that we are pardoned; and it is in dying that we are born to eternal life.

And at the Very End

Have the group assess the learning that they have gained in the session.

• What did you learn?
• Identify any new insights you gained.
• What issues discussed in the session would you like to know more about?

Holding up Half the Sky

A major concern in developing countries has been the improvement of agricultural production and better utilization of available rural resources. Until recently planners have failed to see the dichotomy between their own plans and actual rural needs. Rural development should lead to economic growth for the welfare of all the people. For many underdeveloped countries, it has led to growth for a small minority. In particular, women have been excluded from many programs, with planners rarely giving women's needs more than a cursory glance. Yet, if development is the improvement of human welfare, women should be directly involved in that process.

An important question is: What can women do for rural development? Their talents and contributions to the process can be invaluable. But, even more importantly, what can development do for women? Women in many countries are restricted from participation in all areas of political, economic, and social activities by legal and cultural barriers. They are ignored in decision-making processes of rural development planning, and their needs are rarely known or addressed. Essentially, women are powerless: unable to shape their own lives and unable to choose how they want to live. Women in many developing countries feel not only physical anguish from overwork and undernourishment, but also mental anguish from their inability to control their own lives.

The social, structural, attitudinal, and technical changes that have occurred in rural development and land use programs have, for the most part, put women at a disadvantage vis-à-vis the rest of society. Changes in the traditional systems of social organization and production in rural areas have disrupted complementary roles of women and men and the sharing of responsibilities between them. It has altered the traditional division of labor at women's expense, pushing them out of their traditional economic activities and widening the productivity gap between their labor and that of men.

In traditional societies of Africa, women were often much better off. In West African preindustrial societies, women had a position of power. They were important agricultural producers, who controlled the types of crops raised and the way the crops were raised. With colonial rule, the status of women began to deteriorate. Along with political and economic rule, the West brought its own definition of women's roles. Colonial policies were aimed at improving and modernizing the farming systems, changing them to export crop enterprises. It was felt that female farming was inferior to male farming. Improvement in agriculture required that men take over production. In Uganda, women had traditionally cultivated cotton. In 1923, the European Director of Agriculture stated that "cotton growing could not be left to women and old people." A decade later, men were growing cotton and coffee, and male laborers were being imported to work during harvest time. This type of policy undermined the position of women.

Not only were women replaced by men in farming, but subsistence crops were replaced by cash crops, leaving less land for growing food crops. To encourage men to grow cash crops or to take jobs on plantations, colonial governments frequently introduced taxes, forcing men into the money economy, while women remained without access to income.

With men drawn into the modern sector, women acquired tasks that were formerly men's work. Not only did women have to grow food for family consumption and perform household activities, they also had to perform additional activities such as hunting and livestock care. Women were not given access to technical improvements in farming even as they had to grow food on less land with less help. Consequently, women experienced a decline in food productivity. Since their status had been based on their ability to produce for their families, a decline in productivity meant a decline in social status.

Formal colonialism is now dead, but it has left an indelible imprint on each society that it has touched. The pattern of indigenous production and trade relationships have been dramatically affected. Development programs since colonialism have often followed similar patterns emphasizing export crops and "modernization." This has had a continuing impact on rural women in particular.

Rural women are still largely responsible for food production in developing countries. Women usually work more hours per day and more days per week than men, working eighteen to twenty hours at times, while men work twelve hours or less per day. Also, with male migration to urban areas continuing, work formerly done by men must now be done by women. The result is that women do at least half and in some cases 70 to 80 percent of all agricultural work in many countries. Even in the southern part of the Sahara, where men did most of the cultivation during the early part of the century, female farming is now predominant. This is all the more remarkable since this area is not exclusively devoted to subsistence production.

Even though they have a heavy share of the agricultural work, women receive little or no training in new farming methods. In the Upper Volta, agricultural schools are not open to women, though 80 percent of the farming is done by women. These restrictions are detrimental to the economy because they prevent agricultural productivity from increasing and prohibit rural incomes from rising. Since women are then often able to produce only enough food for family consumption, they have no surplus to sell for income. The inevitable result is that women are discouraged from participating in agriculture and are not likely to produce more than enough for their families.

Men are taught new techniques, but it is for export crops that these are taught. Export crops are supported by systematic research and government investment, while food crops are favored by few such programs. Men use earnings to improve production, while women have no incomes to finance improvements. This enhances the prestige of men and lowers that of women. Men represent modern farming in the village, women represent old drudgery.

Even land reform has often had negative effects on women cultivators. In countries where women are growing their own crops on communally held lands, they may lose their rights to produce when private ownership is introduced and men—as family heads—are given title. In the Bikiti Reserve in Zimbabwe, a traditionally female farming area, the land tenure changes of 1957 allocated land to men and widows only. This meant that 23 percent of those who received land were absent men who worked as wage laborers outside the region, while their wives lived as cultivators in the reserve. The women's position became even more precarious, because men could and did divorce their wives and marry again, and ex-wives were deprived of the land they had worked for years.

To ensure that women are integrated into rural development, women need to be included in agricultural training programs. Additionally, their tenure rights need to be protected. When this happens, there will be the chance for women to benefit more from their labors. For example, between 1970 and 1973, eleven special seminars were organized in East African countries to teach improved use of available foods and new techniques in health care. Where training has been directed at women, definite increases in productivity have been noted.

Technology can also be introduced to save household labor. Sewage systems and piped water could cut labor time tremendously. Mechanical grinders would help in the preparation of food. In Kenya, the introduction of tin roofs relieved women from the heavy burden of constantly going to the well for water, since water could be collected from the roof. There is a need for women to be educated about nutrition and the preservation of foods. Food canning could be a high priority, and more efficient ways of drying food would be helpful. With better food preparation techniques, women could market their surpluses more easily.

Agricultural training will not be as productive if women do not have the capital necessary to make improvements. In Zambia, for the last six years, women have been trained in all agricultural subjects and hired equally with men, but married women cannot get loans. Credit could be made available for improving production and for buying small technology, such as pumps for irrigation, or seeds. Credit could even be automatically extended when a farmer has attended an agricultural extension course, since this would ensure that the knowledge would be applied in practice.

If women had access to capital, land, and new agricultural methods, their productivity would increase. Their surplus could then be sold and incomes would begin to rise. This would not only begin to bridge the gap between men and women, but also between rural and urban areas. This gap leads to an exodus from rural areas to the cities in the search for employment.

For women in developing countries in particular, exclusion from rural development has meant deprivation and hardship. If their needs are ignored, truly just and sustainable land use systems cannot be developed. Ignoring those holding up half the sky prevents the whole society from using its resources fully or equitably. The challenge of meeting women's needs is part of the struggle for meaningful rural development and new designs for land use systems.

Bibliography

Beck, Lois, and Keddie, Nikki. *Women in the Muslim World*. Cambridge, Mass.: Harvard University Press, 1978.

Boserup, Ester. *Integration of Women in Development*. New York: United Nations Development Programme, May 1975.

Boserup, Ester. *Women's Role in Economic Development*. New York: St. Martin's Press, 1970.

George, Susan. *How the Other Half Dies*. Montclair, N.J.: Allanheld, Osmun and Co., 1977.

Dixon, Ruth. "Women's Rights and Fertility." *Reports on Population Family Planning, January 1975.* New York, Population Council, 1975.

Huston, Perdita. "Power and Pregnancy." *New Internationalist,* 52 (June 1977).

Lappe, Frances Moore, and Collins, Joseph. *Food First*. New York: Ballantine Books, 1979.

Mamdani, Mahmood. *The Myth of Population Control: Family, Caste, and Class in an Indian Village*. New York: Monthly Review.

Newland, Kathleen, and McGrath, Patricia. *The Sisterhood of Man*. New York: W.W. Norton and Co., 1979.

Tinker, Irene, and Bramsen, Bo. *Women and World Development*. Washington, D.C.: Overseas Development Council, 1976.

Wingspread Workshop. *Women and World Development*. Racine, Wisc.: The Johnson Foundation, 1976.

World Bank. *Women and Development*. Washington, D.C.: World Bank, 1975.

Youssef, Nadia. *Women and Work in Developing Societies*. Population Monograph Series, no. 15. Berkeley: University of California Press, 1975.

SELECTION A
WOMEN'S LIBERATION REACHES INTO THE WORLD'S VILLAGES

by Julia Malone

Reprinted from *The Christian Science Monitor,* July 21, 1980

Political squabbling among the nations may have stolen center stage here at the World Conference of the United Nations Decade for Women. But disputes over Palestine and South Africa have not been able to hide the fact also brought out in this 136-nation gathering:

That the "liberation" once dismissed as the hobby of upper-middle-class women has matured into a worldwide movement. It is beginning to reach into the poorest countires and into the tiniest villages. More and more women are getting at least the first elements of an education, are learning how to earn money themselves, how to limit the size of their families.

One specific achievement of the conference was the signing July 17 by 51 countries of a Convention on the Elimination of All Forms of Discrimination Against Women. If ratified by signing nations, the convention will commit them to equal pay, maternity benefits, help for rural women, and fair credit laws.

Moreover, the convention calls for a watchdog committee to check on progress. The agreement, approved by the UN General Assembly last December, now has a total of 62 signatories (including the US), four of whom have already ratified.

The convention is a clear evidence that "attitudes have changed," comments Sarah Weddington, who co-chairs the US delegation along with UN Ambassador Donald McHenry.

But beyond the debates here and the signing of the convention, perhaps the changing status of women is best seen through the experiences of some of the 900 women delegates (out of a total 1,200 delegates) attending.

Begum Taslima Abed, head of the Bangladesh delegation, serves her country's parliament. Bangladesh is a land where only 9 percent of the women and 33 percent of the men can read and write. And soon after the UN Decade for Women was declared at the first World Conference for Women in Mexico City in 1975, the extremely poor South Asian nation began to look at its women's role. Like many other third-world nations, it set up a Women's Affairs Division.

Now Mrs. Abed is state minister for women's affairs and she has a vision for the women of her country. Bangladesh must take its women into account, she says. "We are a great force. One half of the population is women. If this half is left behind, the country cannot develop."

Bringing Bangladesh women into development has not been easy. Mrs. Abed says that the typical rural farm wife begins her day before sunrise and consumes much of her time walking to the distant river to wash and to collect the daily water supply. She feeds her family rice, that she must refine by a primitive hand process, and bread from wheat that she has ground herself.

In the late afternoons, however, the village women are beginning to join a new "self-reliant program," says Mrs. Abed. Here they learn weaving and how to raise goats and ducks as well as how to use birth control. Independence is the key, says Mrs. Abed. "In economic independence you get honor." Her hope for the next half of the decade is for more vocational education for women.

The new interest in women has made a difference in Kenya as well, says Rose Waruhiu, a member of the Kenyan delegation. Kenya now has a Women's Bureau, and she sees more awareness of women's views.

Before 1975, "The consciousness was not there," she says. "The men thought they were doing well until they saw that they should be consulting the women on the farms."

Today the Kenyan government has set a goal to provide water to every household by the end of the century, an achievement that would most benefit women since they traditionally make the often long hikes to fetch water.

Although an international movement of women is apparent at this gathering of women from around the globe, it is equally evident that change is coming in different forms. Just as the dress of the participants ranges from tailored Western dress to India saris, long African dresses, and Islamic head covers, the new roles of women are coming in different forms.

At the unofficial Non-Governmental Organization (NGO) forum, a few miles from the official UN conference, the Iranian delegation has set up a display in defense of the Islamic revolution and the return to wearing the chador (strict Islamic veil). But included in the display is a poster of a woman in a black chador wielding a machine gun.

"Most women want to wear the chador," explains an Iranian delegate who adds that she herself now is beginning to wear the traditional garb for the first time.

A Danish woman asserts that child-rearing is for both men and women— "My husband is taking care of my children now."

A Pakistani woman tells of her successful architect daughter who lives with a husband whom she had never met before the wedding. Arranged marriages are best, says the mother, whose own marriage has lasted 33 years. She says that her daughter is still an "Asian woman" in her outlook.

Session 6

POPULATION

Bible Study and Discussion

Genesis 1:1–2:4
Matthew 10:32–42

- Read and discuss the Scriptural passages.
- Discuss the passages "to rule" (Gen. 1:26) and "Be fruitful and increase . . . subdue it . . ." (Gen. 1:28).
- Compare Genesis 1:1–2:4 with Genesis 2:5–25. Do you discern a different concept of the purpose of human history in these two accounts of creation?
- If Christians place Christ first among all earthly considerations, as the Matthew reading suggests, does this affect our social, political, and economic relationships?

Moving Along

- Do you think the earth can sustain the population projected for the year 2000?
- Is hunger and malnutrition the result of inadequate food production, distribution, or education?
- How many pounds of food, meat, dairy, and grain, do you think you eat in one year?
- Do Farb and Armelagos convince you in "The Food Connection" (Selection A, pp. 74–80) that ". . . if the question is asked whether mechanized producers are extracting from the soil a greater number of calories of food in proportion to the calories of energy they expend, the answer is no"? Discuss.
- In his address before the National Ocean Industries Association (Selection B, pp. 80–86), Mr. Secretary Pickering said: ". . . sentiment also is growing in Congress, industry, and the regional

councils to use U.S. fish allocations as devices or bargaining chips to open foreign markets to U.S. fisheries exports and to gain other economic benefits in the fisheries arena.'' Given the context of this statement and in light of the discussion around the biblical passages above, how do you view this ''sentiment'' about the use of fish as ''devices or bargaining chips''?

Preparing for the Next Session

- Identify a moderator for the next meeting.
- Suggest that the participants read the essay and articles for Session 7: Land Marginalization.
- Since the next session deals with land development, survey the group and ask for volunteers to report back on the development of land in your area within the past ten years.

Ending

- Read aloud:
    Revelation 8:6–9:21
- Pause for silent meditation and reflection.
- Share prayers or litanies prepared by participants.
- Read (or sing):
    Hymn 295

Lord of all majesty and might,
    Whose presence fills the unfathomed deep,
Wherein uncounted worlds of light
    Through countless ages vigil keep;
        Eternal God, can such as we,
        Frail mortal men, know aught of thee?

Beyond all knowledge thou art wise,
    With wisdom that transcends all thought:
Yet still we seek with straining eyes,
    Yea, seek thee as our fathers sought;
        Nor will we from the quest depart
        Till we shall know thee as thou art.

Frail though our form, and brief our day,
    Our mind has bridged the gulf of years,
Our puny magnitude of starry spheres:
        Within us is eternity;
        Whence comes it, Father, but from thee?

For, when thy wondrous works we scan,
  And Mind gives answer back to mind,
Thine image stands revealed in man;
  And, seeking, he shall surely find.
    Thy sons, our heritage we claim:
    Shall not thy children know thy Name?

We know in part: enough we know
  To walk with thee, and walk aright;
And thou shalt guide us as we go,
  And lead us into fuller light,
    Till, when we stand before thy throne,
    We know at last as we are known.

G. W. BRIGGS, 1933

·   Read aloud:

Prayers of the People

Deacon or other leader

Let us pray for the Church and for the world.

Grant, Almighty God, that all who confess your Name may be united in your truth, live together in your love, and reveal your glory in the world.

Silence

Lord, in your mercy
Hear our prayer.

Guide the people of this land, and of all the nations, in the ways of justice and peace; that we may honor one another and serve the common good.

Silence

Lord, in your mercy
Hear our prayer.

Give us all a reverence for the earth as your own creation, that we may use its resources rightly in the service of others and to your honor and glory.

Silence

Lord, in your mercy
Hear our prayer.

Bless all whose lives are closely linked with ours, and grant that we may serve Christ in them, and love one another as he loves us.

Silence

Lord, in our mercy
Hear our prayer.

Comfort and heal all those who suffer in body, mind, or spirit; give them courage and hope in their troubles, and bring them the joy of your salvation.

Silence

Lord, in your mercy
Hear our prayer.

We commend to your mercy all who have died, that your will for them may be fulfilled; and we pray that we may share with all your saints in your eternal kingdom.

Silence

Lord, in your mercy
Hear our prayer.

The Celebrant adds a concluding Collect.

Almighty and eternal God, ruler of all things in heaven and earth: Mercifully accept the prayers of your people, and strengthen us to do your will; through Jesus Christ our Lord.

And at the Very End

Have the group assess the learning they have gained in the session.
- What did you learn?
- Identify any new insights you gained.
- What issues discussed in the session would you like to know more about?

Population

Over the past two decades, as communication technologies have brought the nations of the world closer together, vacillating and often conflicting predictions of demographers, sociologists, and futurists have confused us about the problems of a burgeoning world population and its capacity to sustain itself. The inevitable conflict between population and food supply was anticipated in the late eighteenth century by the far-sighted English social scientist, Thomas Malthus, who warned that population growth would increase geometrically, while food production could increase only arithmetically. Almost two centuries later, however, we are faced with the fact that the variables that have created the gap between the supply of the world's food and the demand are far more complex than Malthus's formula suggests. The questions raised by the current situation are basic but very difficult to answer. Is there really such a thing as a population explosion? Can we blame the rapid multiplication of the world's population for the malnutrition and hunger that plagues at least 10 percent of the world's 4 billion people or are the factors of land distribution, land degradation, and failing social and economic development actually the culprits? If population growth is at the bottom of the vicious cycle of poverty, is there anything that can be done about it, in light of the many barriers to effective family planning programs?

To give us a sense of how critical the present situation is, it is helpful to view population growth in an historical context. A time line best portrays the evolution of the trend. From A.D. 1 to 1750, the world population increased 150 percent, and in the upcoming decades it will double every forty-one years. Historically, we have no experience with such astounding rates of growth; and there is no certainty, even among experts, about what the far-reaching effects will be and how we can cope with them. These figures, however, demonstrate something of the impossibility, mathematically speaking, of the continuance of the current trend. At the same time, we know that present rates of growth are certain to affect future generations of at least one hundred years. Stated simply, the faster the population grows, the younger the average age of the population becomes, thus creating an age structure that allows more women in the childbearing ages to have more children more quickly. A momentum is built in, as we have experienced in the United States as a result of the "baby boom."

Behind the striking reality demonstrated on the time line is another dimension of the problem—the burden of the population growth has shifted from the developed to the developing world. *The Preliminary Report of the Presidential Commission on World Hunger* states:

> Over 4.2 billion people inhabit the world today, 3 billion of them in the developing countries. World population is growing at the rate of 70–80 million per year, with the developing countries

accounting for 86% of the increase. These figures mean that by the year 2000 the world's population will total at least 6 billion, and nearly 8 out of 10 people will live in the developing world.

Up until the twentieth century, the growth rates of the industrialized nations far surpassed those of the developing countries. The shift is due primarily to the lowering of death rates in these countries, which occurred as a result of medical and public health technologies imported from the developed world after the Second World War. At the same time that mortality rates have plummeted, the fertility rates have remained very high. In demographic terms, it is said that these nations have not yet undergone the "demographic transition," which the United States and nations of Western Europe experienced in the early twentiety century. The demographic transition is defined as the shift from high birth rates and declining death rates, yielding high growth rates to controlled birth rates and low death rates, usually resulting in declining growth. Many ethical questions are raised in retrospect, as we realize the role that public health improvements and new technologies transported to lesser-developed countries have played in bringing about the unprecedented population growth occurring in these nations today. Unfortunately, changes in the social, economic, and political structures, such as increased educational and employment opportunities for women and government policies that encourage the postponement of marriage and small families, have not accompanied the decline in death rates brought to third world countries from the outside. The peoples' motivation to have large families is fostered not only by the prevailing system of subsistence agriculture, in which children are viewed as irreplaceable and very economical laborers, but also by many existing religious systems which require mothers to bear many sons in order to assure the preservation of the paternal line.

Pleas for population control call in to question a principle of family life that was dear to Old Testament characters such as Abraham and Sarah and continues to be important to many today—the privilege of carrying out God's call to his people to be fruitful and multiply. For many in the United States, cries for population control have meant transferring considerations such as "How many children can we afford to have?" from the realm of individual decision-making to the arena of social responsibility: "How many children of ours can the world's limited resources afford to sustain?" Although zero population growth is an admirable goal in terms of preserving the earth's resources, it is not acceptable to most nations and to many religious and ethnic communites. Individual choices about the size of one's family are often influenced by government or religious officials; and within third world countries decisions about childbearing are often not in the hands of the childbearers themselves. Furthermore, even when parents do plan the size of their own families, it does not necessarily lead to national population control. In Africa, for example, it has been found that most women's desired family size is greater than the number of children they are actually able to have and keep alive. Yet the population growth across the continent is 2.64 percent per year.

We can talk about disproportionate population growth in the third world only as we talk about the disproportionate use and waste of world resources in the first world. Many believe that it is economic realities, such as the present "hardships" of runaway inflation, the lack of energy self-sufficiency, increasing threats to our health and safety, and the crisis of American agriculture, that are motivating our present low rate of population growth. Developing nations are experiencing hardships of the population–resource squeeze very directly in the form of poor land use, fast growing urbanization, international migration, and increased political instability, yet their response to these hardships is less clear.

In the highlands of the Himalayas, the South American Andes, and East Africa, overpopulation is one factor contributing to the forest depletion and the resultant soil erosion and top-soil washout that have driven people to the lowlands to seek better land and a better life. This movement, in addition to the priorities that governments and outside agencies place on the growth of industry in urban areas, has led to the rapid multiplication of people in cities. Third world cities have been the first recipients of colonial and postcolonial aid, leading to quickly lowered death rates; yet the overcrowded conditions prevent rural migrants from realizing the promise of improved life in the city, and they are forced to bring their rural life with them. A further consequence of overcrowded third world urban areas is what we know as the "brain drain." Those citizens of developing countries who have benefited the most from training at home and abroad are the most likely to leave their own countries, where they cannot be absorbed into the economy and can no longer be satisfied with the standard of living, to work in an industrialized nation.

The problems for developing nations are overwhelming, yet a decline in population growth rates is not necessarily the solution. After examining the best available estimates of trends affecting food supply and demand and nutritional needs through the year 2000, the Presidential Commission on World Hunger determined that the world can produce enough food to feed the population if it is willing to meet the cost. Part of that cost must be paid by the leaders of developing countries as they institute policies that will encouage women's participation in resource development and community-based alternatives to subsistence farming. A good deal of the cost must be paid by developed nations such as the United States as they offer aid to these countries for devising and implementing more effective food production and distribution methods. The developed nations are also obligated to consider the effects that their own food production, distribution, and consumption patterns have on their less-developed neighbors.

It is important to remind ourselves that the world's agricultural systems—dependent on available land, labor, capital, and knowledge—are inextricably tied to local, national, and international economic and political structures that determine what should be produced, where, by whom, and for whom. In turn, agricultural systems are very influential in determining how many children a family needs or wants to have. Families will not decide to have fewer children until they are sure of the advantages of doing so. The ideal, then, is to develop attractive alternatives to large families before the hardship of uncontrolled population growth acts cruelly to cure itself.

SELECTION A
THE FOOD CONNECTION
by Peter Farb and George Armelagos
Reprinted from *Natural History,* September, 1980.

The modern cultural adaptation that emerged first in Britain, then in Western Europe and North America, is now spreading rapidly around the globe—and even penetrating into the lands of remote pastoralists, horticulturists, and hunter-gatherers. Often regarded as synonymous with the Industrial Revolution—which began almost exactly two hundred years ago with James Watt's improved version of the steam engine—modernization entails much more than the replacement of human muscle by energy from machines. It involves developments in the structure of the family, the division of labor, the growth of population, and the environment, as well as diet.

The Industrial Revolution could not have taken place without the agricultural revolution that preceded it and that was based on an increase in production due both to new crops from the Americas and to new methods of farming. Yields of food were increased substantially by such simple techniques as the rotation of crops—a sequence from year to year, for example, of barley, clover, wheat, and turnips, instead of leaving the field fallow when its fertility had been depleted. The selective breeding of cattle also greatly increased the yields of meat and milk. In such ways, what had been an inefficient system of agriculture was eventually replaced by large-scale mechanized farming that took on the character of modern industry. Oliver Goldsmith in his poem *The Deserted Village*—published in 1770, five years before Watt's improved steam engine first came into use—described how the mechanization of agriculture had already forced many farmers to abandon their small holdings and migrate to the cities. This considerable portion of the British population provided the labor for an industrialization that would otherwise have been impossible.

One phenomenon of modernization has been an increasingly rapid rise in population. In 1750 the total population of the world was probably about 750 million, by 1830 it had increased to a billion, by 1930 it was two billion, and by 1975 four billion. In other words, the human species needed millions of years to reach a population of a billion, but thereafter the second billion was added in only a hundred years, the third in thirty years, and the fourth in a mere fifteen years. This growth was long attributed to a drop in the death rate that stemmed from advances in medicine, but some demographers now question whether medicine had much of an effect. Tuberculosis, for example, was the largest single cause of death in Britain in the last century, yet in the fifty years previous to 1882—when the tubercle baccillus was first identified by Robert Koch—deaths caused by it had already declined by about half. Pneumonia, influenza, infectious bronchitis, and other diseases also began significant declines early in the nineteenth century, years before immunization and potent new drugs could have had any effect.

If not medical advances, then what can explain the change in the response to infection by people living in modern societies? The answer seems to be the profound effect of improved nutrition on the body's response to microorganisms. The decline in the death rate that occurred in Europe and in North America during the last century is being witnessed today in developing nations, and has the same probable cause. Well-nourished people have a much lower rate of infection and, even if infected, are much more likely to recover as compared to poorly nourished people. Before the widespread use of the measles vaccine, practically every child in every country caught measles, but three hundred times more deaths occurred in the poorer countries than in the richer ones. The reason was not that the virus was somehow more potent in poor countries or that these lacked medical services, but that in poorly nourished countries the virus attacked children who, because of chronic malnutrition, were less able to resist it.

Along with an improved agriculture came the introduction into Europe of new crops from the Americas, notably white potatoes into northern Europe and maize into southern Europe. In both Spain and Italy, where the cultivation of maize was widespread, populations soared—nearly doubling in Spain and increasing from eleven to eighteen million in Italy between the beginning and the end of the eighteenth century. The potato was not accepted so readily in Europe, even though it had been cultivated in the Andean highlands of Peru for about 2,500 years. It was at first regarded with suspicion, in part because it was grown from a tuber rather than from seeds, as were all other edible plants in Europe up to that time. But by the beginning of the eighteenth century, the potato had become a common food for peasants, who found in it the perfect crop for small parcels of arable land. Just one acre planted to potatoes could feed a family of five or six, plus a cow or pig, for most of a year. The plant could grow in a wide variety of soils, and it required no tools other than a spade and a hoe. It matured within three or four months, as compared to the well over half a year required for grain crops, and it had the advantage of a high nutritional value.

The most dramatic effect of the potato's introduction into Europe was seen in Ireland. By the middle of the eighteenth century, most of the Irish population was subsisting almost exclusively on potatoes, and Ireland's perennially recurring famines appeared at last to be ended. Potatoes do not have aphrodisiac powers, as was once believed, but they did contribute to the sudden increase in the Irish population, making large families possible because they provided a maximum of sustenance with a minimum of labor. The population of Ireland grew from just above three million in 1754 to more than eight million in 1845. Then a blight struck, bringing about the Great Potato Famine that was to last four years.

An increase in population as a result of new foods rather than of industrialization and medical advances also took place in China. The sweet potato, long grown by South American Indians, was early imported as a crop into China and was established by 1594, when it provided sustenance at a time when the native grains were succumbing to drought. An eighteenth-century agricultural commentary extolled sweet potatoes as a versatile crop that could be boiled, ground, or fermented; could be fed to animals, as well as to humans; and could grow where grains did not survive. By that century, other New World crops were being widely grown: maize was allowing people from the crowded Yangtze region to migrate inland and farm drier lands; the white potato made it possible to bring into production lands that were too impoverished even for growing maize; and peanuts could be grown in the previously useless soils along rivers and streams. The new crops allowed a Chinese population that had reached the limits of its previous resources to begin a new spurt in growth. The numbers expanded from about 150 million people in the early 1700s to about 450 million only a century and a half later. The worldwide growth in population over the past several centuries is similar to what occurred in China, and can be assumed to have occurred for similar reasons. As soon as food resources could be moved from continent to continent because of the invention of long-distance transportation, a surge in population took place, one that had little to do with industrialization, shorter work hours, or advances in the practice of medicine.

People in modern societies usually assume that their own kind of mechanized agriculture is the most efficient known. But if the question is asked whether mechanized producers are really extracting from the soil a greater number of calories of food in proportion to the calories of energy they expend, the answer is no. In fact, they are very inefficient in this regard when compared with other adaptations—as is shown by a simple equation developed by anthropologist Marvin Harris that makes it possible to analyze the efficiency of any system for providing food energy:

$$\frac{E}{m \times t \times r} = e$$

That is, a society's annual production of food energy, E (as expressed in thousands of calories, or kilocalories), divided by the number of food producers (m), times the hours each works at food production during the year (t), times the calories expended per producer each hour in doing the work (r) equals e, that society's techno-environmental efficiency (in other words, the calories produced for each calorie of energy expended). Obviously, e must be greater than one because no society can survive for very long unless it produces more energy than it expends; actually, the value of e must be substantially higher than one to provide for such nonproducing activities as toolmaking, ceremonials, and recreation, among other things, and also to support the young, the elderly, the sick, and other nonproducers in the society. The larger e becomes, therefore, the greater is the society's techno-environmental efficiency in producing food energy above the amount it expends.

In a hunting-gathering society, such as the San, or Bushmen, of the Kalahari Desert, the equation is applied by Marvin Harris (using data collected by Richard Lee) as follows: A camp of twenty adults (m), each working 805 hours a year (t) and expending 150 calories per hour (r), to produce 23,000,000 kilocalories annually (E), has an efficiency of 9.5 (e)—which means that the San are producing between nine and ten calories for each calorie of energy expended.

This low efficiency does not allow much of a margin of safety and is insufficient to provide food for full-time specialists such as woodcarvers or priests. But the San cannot increase their efficiency because the average expenditure per producer of 150 calories an hour cannot be raised substantially; the human body simply cannot withstand long periods of being overheated or out of breath (which is why the average value for r of 150 remains the same in all of the adaptations to be discussed here). For each adult in the camp to work more than 805 hours a year (an average of a mere two hours or so a day) would not solve the problem because the San can neither transport nor store a surplus, and any increased effort would quickly deplete the food resources around the camp. They might try to enlarge the population of their camp to increase the number of producers, but the food supply in the Kalahari Desert is insufficient to support dense populations that lack the knowledge and tools to build irrigation dams. So long as the San follow their traditional ways, they obviously can do almost nothing to increase their techno-environmental efficiency.

Nor would it be possible for the San to switch to horticulture, given both the harsh environment and their limited technology for overcoming it. Even if they could, Marvin Harris has shown, using energy data from a horticultural village in Gambia, West Africa, how little would be gained. Instead of the 20 food producers in the San camp, this Gambian village had 334, as well as a better climate for plant growth and a more complex technology. Yet the application of the equation shows an efficiency only slightly above that of the San. For an annual production of 460,000,000 kilocalories, 334 persons, each working 820 hours annually and expending 150 calories an hour, produce a little over 11 calories for each calorie of expended energy.

The main advantage of horticulture over hunting-gathering is not its much greater efficiency but rather that people can live together in larger and more permanent settlements. The denser population of a sedentary village allows for protection against enemies and gives greater opportunity for cultural interaction.

Detailed energy data do not exist for pastoral peoples, but their efficiency is believed to be no greater than for hunter-gatherers and horticulturists. It may indeed be less, since to allow domesticated animals to eat plant foods and then to eat the animal or its milk and blood takes the process of production through an extra step, with a loss of calories along the way. This assumption seems supported by the few studies that have been made. For one tribe of southern Tunisia that herds sheep and goats and also practices a little horticulture, anthropologist William Bedoian has calculated a techno-environmental efficiency of about six; for some Indians in the Andes of South America who are almost exclusively pastoralists, R. Brooke Thomas has determined the figure to be a little more than two.

Figures on efficiency under other adaptations do not increase by much until the complex level of irrigation agriculture is reached. This adaptation can feed more people on less land than any other, including mechanized agriculture. Over the millenniums, it has developed most notably in eastern Asia because of particular conditions prevailing there: many people to provide the labor for building and maintaining irrigation works, abundant water, and a shortage of arable land. As the irrigation system develops and production is intensified, more and more people are fed from the same amount of land—although at the price of increasing the amount of labor per unit of land, which means that the land must be worked ever more intensively by more people. Given this cycle, no one can become richer by working harder because the payments allocated to labor must be divided among a larger and larger force. And since such systems can develop only in the presence of an autocratic government, any economic growth that occurs is inevitably siphoned off by the bureaucratic elite that exists outside of the energy system.

A detailed study of labor inputs and food yields for an irrigation village in Yunnan Province, China, before the fall of the Nationalist government shows a greatly increased techno-environmental efficiency over hunting-gathering, horticulture, and pastoralism. Four hundred eighteen persons, each working

1,129 hours annually, produced 3,788,000,000 kilocalories, resulting in between 53 and 54 calories produced for each calorie of energy expended. A higher efficiency, it should be noted, does not produce an increase in leisure, as is often supposed. Rather, each producer must work harder—in fact, some 35 percent more labor was performed by each of these Chinese than by each of the San.

Of the nearly four billion kilocalories produced annually by this Chinese village, the villagers were estimated to need no more than a sixth of that amount. What happened, then, to the more than three billion kilocalories they produced each year over what they consumed? The surplus was used to feed the scores of millions in Chinese towns and cities who did not participate directly in food production, was sent to market and exchanged for manufactured goods, or was taken away in the form of taxes levied by the local, provincial, and national governments and in the form of rent payments to large landowners.

Modern societies are too complex to be analyzed by the equation employed here, but a few generalizations can be made. Once again, it is a mistake to suppose that modern societies allow people to work less hard for their daily bread. Out of the 1,129 hours worked by one Chinese irrigation farmer in a year, only 122 were needed to grow enough food to sustain that farmer. A blue-collar worker in the United States, on the other hand, spends 180 hours earning enough money to purchase a year's supply of food. Notwithstanding Western notions of the Chinese peasants' incessant labor, it is plain that they actually need to work less by a third than North Americans or Europeans to keep themselves supplied with food. Moreover, although a mechanized farmer in the American Midwest need put in an annual total of only nine hours of work for each acre to achieve an astounding 6,000 calories for each calorie of effort, that figure ignores the enormous amounts of human labor that go into manufacturing and transporting the trucks, tractors, combines, fuel, fertilizer, pesticides, fence wire, and everything else used by the farmer, not to mention transporting the food itself. For every person who actually works on a Midwestern farm, the labor of at least two others off the farm is needed to supply equipment and services directly to the farmer—aside from the very many more whose labors contribute indirectly to the final product. Altogether, a total of 2,790 calories of energy must be expended to produce and deliver to a consumer in the United States just one can of corn providing a total of 270 calories. The production of meat entails an even greater deficit: an expenditure of 22,000 calories is needed to produce the somewhat less than four ounces of beefsteak that also provides 270 calories.

In short, present-day agriculture is much less efficient than traditional irrigation methods that have been used by Asians, among others, in this century and by Mayas, Mesopotamians, Egyptians, and Chinese in antiquity. The primary advantage of mechanized agriculture is that it requires the participation of fewer farmers, but for that, the price paid in machines, fossil fuels, and other expenditures of energy is enormous. A severe price is also paid in human labor. Once the expensive machines have been manufactured and deployed on the farms, they are economically efficient only if operated throughout the daylight hours, and indeed farmers in the United States often labor for sixteen hours a day. The boast of industrialized societies that they have decreased the workload is valid only in comparison with the exploitation of labor that existed in the early decades of the Industrial Revolution. If the prevailing forty-hour work week of North America and Europe were proposed to the San, whoever did so would be considered to be exploitive, inhuman, or plain mad.

SELECTION B
OCEAN DEVELOPMENT IN THE 1980s
by Thomas R. Pickering
Assistant Secretary for Oceans and International Environmental and Scientific Affairs

It is a pleasure to be with you at your Eighth Annual Meeting. Your theme, "The 1980s: Decade for Ocean Development," is timely and places you in good company. As you know, last year 53 Members of the Congress broached the concept of the 1980s as a decade of ocean resource use and management in a letter to the President. The idea is now under study by the Administration and by the presidentially appointed National Advisory Committee on Oceans and Atmosphere.

By whatever name we give to these endeavors—whether it be the decade of ocean development, the decade of ocean resource use and management, or a name yet to be coined—I believe we are all striving to attain a common goal. That goal is the development of marine resources, through the encouragement of private enterprise, in a manner that protects the marine environment and equitably accommodates the often competing demands on ocean space.

Certainly, that is a principal goal of the bureau which I head in the Department of State—the Bureau of Oceans and International Environmental and Scientific Affairs. We are charged with handling a wide variety of international oceans issues pertinent to your theme. These include fisheries negotiations and ocean management matters concerned with marine scientific research, marine mammals, marine pollution, and polar affairs. We also have responsibilities with regard to the third U.N. Conference on the Law of the Sea, which is presently meeting at the United Nations in New York. At the conclusion of the Law of the Sea Conference, my bureau will be responsible for the foreign policy followup and implementation.

During the past year we have been engaged in an analysis of likely trends and related national objectives in ocean affairs during the 1980s. I would like to share with you some of our thoughts on these matters, particularly as they relate to the development and management of ocean resources. I look forward to your comments on our analysis in the discussion period after these remarks.

We see that, whether or not a law-of-the-sea treaty is concluded, principles

Published by the United States Department of State, Bureau of Public Affairs, Editorial Division.

are evolving that will be applicable to the development and management of ocean resources. Chief among these is the growing trend toward coastal state control over exploring, exploiting, conserving, and managing both the living and nonliving resources of the seabed, subsoil, and superjacent waters out to 200 nautical miles from the coast. Coastal state control over other activities such as the production of energy from the water and winds would also be asserted. Because most of the presently exploitable resources of the oceans are found within 200 nautical miles of the coast, during the 1980s the majority of ocean resource activities will be carried out under the regulation and control of national governments, although we in the State Department will necessarily be involved because of the potential for dispute and conflict which these activities could engender.

Fisheries

The ocean resource activity with which the Department of State has had the longest association is fishing. Since the 1940s the Department has been concerned with the development and management of the living resources of the oceans as an important world source of protein. Looking ahead to the decade of the 1980s, we foresee a declining per capita world fisheries harvest. Despite a marked increase in investment in fishing fleets since 1970, the annual world catch has increased little beyond 70 million tons. At the same time the world's population continues to grow apace.

During the 1980s maximum sustainable yields will have been reached or surpassed in many regions unless more sophisticated management schemes are instituted to rebuild stocks. Better management might actually reduce world catch over the short run as overfishing in some regions is cut, but the end result should be a higher sustained catch over the longer term as depleted stocks recover. An increase in the world catch to 80 million tons by the year 2000 is a possibility. We also see a trend through the 1980s away from long-distance fishing fleets, as coastal states extend their control. Increased emphasis will be placed on new coastal fishing vessels and domestic shore-based or offshore processing operations.

We expect U.S. fisheries policy to continue to be set by the Fishery Conservation and Management Act of 1976, which established our 200-nautical-mile fishery conservation zone. Under the terms of that act, regional fishery management councils initiate the calculation of the optimum yield from each fishery, and determine how much U.S. vessels are capable of harvesting. The Department of State allocates the balance to other nations with which we have governing international fishery agreements. In the past, the primary factor in the Department's determination of allocations has been the traditional or historical levels of foreign fishing.

However, sentiment also is growing in Congress, industry, and the regional councils to use U.S. fish allocations as devices or bargaining chips to open foreign markets to U.S. fisheries exports and to gain other economic benefits in the fisheries arena. We share this interest. As an example, we are now carrying on consultations with Congress, the Commerce Department, and industry prior to reallocating some 350,000 tons of fish we withheld from the

Soviet Union in our reaction to the Soviet invasion of Afghanistan. These consultations will establish the basis for reallocation of this resource, including how we can use it to promote the exports of our own fish.

The Fishery Conservation and Management Act has encouraged significant new investment in the U.S. harvesting and processing capacity. During the 1980s we expect to see a continuing decline in the level of foreign fishing off our coasts. This will reduce the occasions to negotiate additional governing international fishery agreements except in cases where there are opportunities for either reciprocal access by U.S. vessels or where there is a potential for increased economic benefit in the U.S. fisheries sector, such as establishing new joint ventures and increased foreign trade. During the 1980s we will also be giving priority to negotiating arrangements with other countries to help maintain U.S. access to important distant water fisheries such as tuna and shrimp.

Mineral Resources

Turning from fish to mineral resources, during the past decade exploration for petroleum and natural gas from ocean areas has increased dramatically. The search for hydrocarbons on the continental shelf has accelerated at a pace that has exceeded all expectations. However, management of the increased recovery of petroleum from the continental shelf should not prove to be as difficult as the management of fisheries. Unless the seaward extension of a boundary between two countries happens to cross an oil pool, cooperative international management arrangements for the production of petroleum should not be necessary. Where the problem of a common pool occurs, a bilateral or multilateral agreement will have to be reached if it is to be exploited efficiently. In certain areas, cooperative arrangements concerning the landing or shipment of oil and gas may be desirable.

The increased exploitation of offshore petroleum in the 1980s will bring greater possibilities of blowouts and other pollution incidents. Of particular interest to my Department are the possible transboundary environmental impacts arising from offshore hydrocarbon development. The massive blowout and oil spill of the Ixtoc well in the Bay of Campeche is an example of the effect upon our nation of the activities on the continental shelf of another. The mutual vulnerability of coastal nations bordering the same body of water points to a clear need to harmonize safety and antipollution measures, including provisions for blowout prevention, control, and liability.

Working in close cooperation with other agencies such as the Coast Guard, the Department of Energy, and the Department of the Interior, we expect during the 1980s to negotiate with our neighboring nations new and additional contingency planning and other environmental agreements concerning offshore hydrocarbon development. Such initial agreements may well also serve as a precedent for the negotiation of minimum safety and environmental standards within a broader international context. Our long-term goal will be the development of an internationally agreed upon policy for offshore resource activities which have possible transboundary impacts.

Antarctic Resources

Interest in ocean resources have directed man's attention to the farthest frontiers of our planet. The ongoing discussions within the Antarctic Treaty system to develop regimes for the management of the living resources in Antarctic waters and of Antarctica's mineral resources—primarily offshore hydrocarbons—testify to this interest. The United States has taken the lead in seeking solutions to these resource issues. Our objectives for this decade involve:

- Maintaining the Antarctic Treaty system which has successfully reserved Antarctica for peaceful purposes as an arena of free scientific research for the past two decades;
- Instituting an effective system of management and harvesting its living resources so that the renewability of these resources and the health of the marine ecosystem of which they are a part will be insured; and
- Developing an international regime to determine the acceptability of possible mineral resource activities in Antarctica and to govern any such activities carried out there.

To achieve these objectives we must find imaginative solutions to differences of view over sovereignty in Antarctica and imaginative approaches to resource management. We are very close now to an agreement on a convention for the conservation of Antarctic marine living resources and have made a good start toward dealing with mineral resources. If we persevere on the basis of experience and in the spirit of the Antarctic Treaty system I believe that we will achieve our goals in both of these important resource areas.

Renewable Energy Resources

Toward the end of the decade of the 1980s, renewable ocean energy sources, such as ocean thermal energy conversion, will become commercially attractive. By the middle 1980s the Department of Energy intends to inaugurate a power plant for ocean thermal energy conversion of about 10 megawatts for experimental and demonstration purposes. Successful demonstrations, combined with ever-increasing oil prices, could make this type of energy conversion a very interesting energy option during the 1990s for countries in a suitable geographic environment, especially if they must import oil for baseload electricity generation. We expect demonstration projects during the 1980s to receive a great deal of attention, especially with respect to their possible environmental impacts and with respect to the international legal regime under which ocean thermal energy conversion is to operate.

Environmental Concerns

In addition to possible injury from offshore energy production, the environmental health of the ocean in the 1980s may be threatened by greater pressures to use the oceans for dumping. Increasing environmental and political objections to the land-based disposal of highly toxic chemical wastes are making at-sea incineration of such wastes more attractive. During 1979, the ocean dumping convention was amended to take account of this emerging technology. Interim technical guidelines were endorsed by the parties at their fourth consultative meeting.

Disposal of nuclear wastes at sea is also likely to become a more visible issue in the 1980s. Quantities of low-level radioactive wastes being dumped at the Organization for Economic Cooperation and Development's north Atlantic site have been increasing yearly, and the United States, while not a dumping country, has advocated proper monitoring and assessment of the site. The possible emplacement of high-level nuclear wastes in the deep seabed is also receiving increased attention. The United States is studying this concept as a backup option to our primary plans for land-based geological disposal of such wastes. But for countries having serious demographic, geographic, geologic, or hydrologic restrictions, the deep seabed option may be the only alternative short of shipping wastes to other nations. As further experimentation and development occur on the concept during the 1980s, international legal and policy issues are certain to arise.

The Department of State will also continue to be involved in the more traditional ocean pollution issues. Repeated accidents involving large supertankers will require us to be concerned with the development of standards which meet the needs of the international community. Because of our strategic interests in the freedom of navigation, the United States wishes to move the international community away from the concept of absolute coastal state control for pollution purposes in the 200-mile zone. We are instead in favor of other means of handling offshore pollution, such as agreements for joint pollution enforcement, contingency plans for containment and cleanup, information exchange regarding shipping, and port entry regulation.

Solving pollution problems resulting from ocean-based activities is, however, only part of the issue. At present, land-based activities are responsible for the bulk of ocean pollution through river runoffs and atmospheric transfers. With the continued growth of coastal populations and increased agricultural and industrial activity, the pressures on the oceans' absorptive capacities from land-based activities will increase.

The Department of State is working with the National Oceanic and Atmospheric Administration (NOAA) to develop methods for comparing strategies for dealing with coastal zone pollution on an international basis. It is essential that monitoring of the marine environment and scientific research to increase our understanding of marine pollution processes be carried out. The National Ocean Pollution Research and Development and Monitoring Planning Act of 1978 designates the NOAA as the lead agency for developing a comprehensive 5-year plan for Federal ocean pollution research and development and monitoring programs. This plan is to be revised and updated at 2-year intervals. In the coming years we expect also to work closely with NOAA and the other Federal agencies in determining how our national marine pollution monitoring, research, and regulation programs might complement similar activities of international organizations.

Rights of Navigation

While coastal nations are consolidating their control over resources within 200 nautical miles of their coasts, these same ocean areas will be used by other nations for navigation. The need to accommodate national and international rights and duties within 200-mile zones will be one of the more difficult tasks facing us in this decade. My Department will work with other Federal agencies in developing national and international regulations safeguarding navigation in areas of resource activity. The negotiating text presently under consideration within the Law of the Sea Conference treats this subject to the satisfaction of the United States.

Another navigation issue which appears to be emerging as a major problem involves the safety of navigation in congested areas, such as international straits or entrances to harbors. These issues may well have to be addressed in international organizations such as the Intergovernmental Maritime Consultative Organization.

Conference on Law of the Sea

As you know, the third U.N. Conference on the Law of the Sea resumed its ninth session in New York on February 27. My bureau, along with Ambassador Richardson [Special Representative of the President for the Law of the Sea Conference] and his interagency team, has worked long and arduously to develop a realistic negotiating posture in the hope of obtaining substantial progress, as we perceive it, in revision I of the Informal Composite Negotiating Text. As many of you are aware, we have tried to draw upon all the varied interests in the United States who will be affected by a comprehensive law-of-the-sea treaty, including, most certainly, the industries represented by your organization.

At this time, while our representatives are deep in intensive negotiation of a terribly lengthy and intricate text, I cannot predict exactly what improvements we can anticipate at the conclusion of this session. Certainly our negotiators have serious concerns with the present text as it applies to the transfer of technology, a subject with which your organization has been so interested. We are hopeful that a number of changes will be accepted by the conference in the area of technology transfer with regard to seabed mining as well as in the related provisions pertaining to voting rights, assured access, financial arrangements, and other topics.

It would be less than candid if I left you with the impression that the United States negotiating team will obtain agreement from the conference on all the positions that we are proposing to protect the economic interests of the United States. We will do our utmost. Our goal is to obtain a treaty that, on balance, will be acceptable to the United States, including the firms represented by the National Oceans Industries Association.

The Senate has already enacted a bill on deep seabed mining and the House has a similar bill before it. Generally, we continue to believe that the legislation should:

- Be transitional or interim, pending international agreement on a regime for the deep seabed;
- Proceed on the legal basis that, notwithstanding future agreement on an international regulatory regime, deep seabed mining is a freedom of the high seas;
- Not contain investment guarantees against financial losses as a consequence of U.S. ratification of an international treaty;
- Provide for effective environmental protection, sound resource management, the safety of life and property at sea, and effective law enforcement;
- Establish an international revenue-sharing fund to be used for the benefit of developing countries;
- Encourage other deep-seabed-mining legislation patterned on our example through the mechanism of reciprocating state recognition of rights;
- Not require that vessels used in the recovery, processing, or transport of hard minerals from the seabed be exclusively constructed in or documented under the laws of the United States;
- Not require processing plants be located in the United States; and
- Not issue licenses or permits for specific mine sites in a manner that could be misinterpreted as assertion of sovereignty over high seas areas on the seabed.

We believe that these elements are not only consistent with the establishment of an effective domestic seabed-mining regime, but also are fully compatible with the goals and position we have espoused in the law-of-the-sea negotiations.

Session 7

LAND
MARGINALIZATION

Bible Study and Discussion

Hosea 2:2–23
Matthew 13:44–52

- Read and discuss the two Bible passages.
- What "warnings" did God give Israel through Hosea?
- Hosea identifies the "lovers" as food, drink, etc.; can you add to the list?
- Can you rewrite Matthew 13:44–52 from a contemporary perspective?

Moving Along

- The essay on "Land Marginalization" (pp. 89–96) raises many theological questions concerning the doctrine of man and his relationship to the whole of creation. Discuss the various theological concepts of this relationship, such as "stewardship," "cocreator," "crown of creation." What are the implications of each?
- What are the forces that cause "land marginalization"? Are these the same forces within human relationships that cause "lower limits of productivity"?
- Are conservation, technology, and progress mutually exclusive? Discuss. Identify areas in which they *have* worked together for the commonweal.
- Read the accompanying articles (pp. 96–99). In Curtis Harnack's article (Selection A), discuss his comment: "I wondered what kind of stewards of the land recent generations had been and what the judgment of future generations might be." In David F. Salisbury's article (Selection B), do you agree that lost acres are becoming harder to replace by technology? Why do you think the farm lobby

helped defeat a House bill that would have authorized a study of land use planning?

Preparing for the Next Session

· Identify the moderator for the next session.
· Ask participants to prepare prayers of concern for sharing at the next meeting.
· Suggest the reading of Rachel Carson's *Silent Spring* (New York: Fawcett, 1977).

Ending

· Read aloud:
  Psalm 66
  Psalm 67
· Pause for silent meditation and reflection.
· Share prayers written by participants.
· Read aloud:

  Eucharistic Prayer C

  In this prayer, the lines in italics are spoken by the People.

  The Celebrant, whether bishop or priest, faces them and sings or says

  The Lord be with you.
  And also with you.

  Lift up your hearts.
  We lift them to the Lord.

  Let us give thanks to the Lord our God.
  It is right to give him thanks and praise.

  Then, facing the Holy Table, the Celebrant proceeds

  God of all power, Ruler of the Universe, you are worthy of glory and praise.
  Glory to you for ever and ever.

  At your command all things came to be: the vast expanse of interstellar space, galaxies, suns, the planets in their courses, and this fragile earth, our island home.
  By your will they were created and have their being.

From the primal elements you brought forth the human race, and blessed us with memory, reason, and skill. You made us the rulers of creation. But we turned against you, and betrayed your trust; and we turned against one another.
Have mercy, Lord, for we are sinners in your sight.

Again and again, you called us to return. Through prophets and sages you revealed your righteous Law. And in the fullness of time you sent your only Son, born of a woman, to fulfill your Law, to open for us the way of freedom and peace
By his blood, he reconciled us.
By his wounds, we are healed.

And therefore we praise you, joining with the heavenly chorus, with prophets, apostles, and martyrs, and with all those in every generation who have looked to you in hope, to proclaim with them your glory, in their unending hymn:

Celebrant and People

Holy, holy, holy Lord, God of power and might, heaven and earth are full of your glory.
     Hosanna in the highest.
Blessed is he who comes in the name of the Lord.
     Hosanna in the highest.

And at the Very End

Have the group assess the learning they have gained in the session.
- What did you learn?
- Identify any new insights you gained.
- What issues discussed in the session would you like to know more about?

Land Marginalization

It has been said that it is the method of land use that determines the hospitality of the land—putting man's role in land development into a responsible perspective. Consideration of just a few facts may aid us in gauging how wise we "environmentally conscious" Americans have been in using the land soundly: The historical exploitation of Oklahoma farmland was followed by the "unhospitable" event of the Dust Bowl; in Iowa, in 1979, soil erosion rates of 21 tons per acre (or 8.7 pounds per square yard) contributed to the decline of certain crop yields; the rearrangement of Los Angeles topography, motivated by real-estate interests and blatant disregard for the natural cycles of the land, results annually in human loss and environmental degradation through floods, fires, mudslides, and avalanches; and increasingly widespread dumping of enormous quantities of extremely toxic waste into land, for example, in Love Canal in New York, is already yielding increases in leukemia and other cancers, which future generations will risk as they plant their gardens on land that is not even of marginal use, but, in fact, is death-inducing. Such a record does not demonstrate skill comparable to our knowledge in land usage—knowledge that should be applied so that all of creation can realize the land's inherent hospitality.

The record of Western civilization, with its characteristic notion of man as separate and superior to the dust from which he came—and to which he will return—has caused far more irreversible environmental destruction than an alternative worldview, which perceives man as a part of the ecosystem, belonging to the chain of being. As Christians raised in a Western country, we sometimes refuse to hear Jesus the Jew pointing to God's great care for his creation and praising the lilies of the field and birds of the air for their harmony within the system, in stark contrast to the people's anxious and grubbing concerns for acquisition and dominion.

Man's free will and ability to be self-reflective have been a misused gift, with repercussions throughout the biosphere. By forcing our wills and technologies upon the land, we have been able to reap outstandingly high yields from not particularly rich land, but only for short periods of time. Naturally resilient land, taxed beyond its normal strength, can fail to rebound. We are slowly realizing that land can be a nonrenewable resource. Approximately 17 million square kilometers (or 4,200 million acres; over half of the humid tropics) are today taken up by nonagricultural grass or savanna lands. With only 8 percent of the earth's total landmass technically and physically capable of supporting agricultural cultivation, it is literally imperative to our continued existence that we optimally maintain "the good earth."

Man's ill use of the land has certainly made it less than maximally productive. Within the past several years, it has become apparent that areas that were long believed to be natural grasslands were not originally so but, in fact, are "derived" savanna lands ruined by ancient man's land utilization and irreversibly unfit for agricultural purposes today. Through our often unthoughtful efforts to replace native plants with cultivated vegetation, as well as through mismanagement of both, man has historically been instrumental in the formation of wastelands and deserts throughout the world.

Marginalization of the comparatively little agricultural land we have is a phenomenon we can ill afford. Technically, the term "land marginalization" refers to the process or act whereby land is reduced to its lower limits of productivity, possibly being rendered completely infertile. It is precipitated by the improper use and overuse of land, with the former being the most frequent cause of unalterable infertility. To arrive at any lasting solutions for preventing irreversible reduction of the land's capacity to produce, we must try to grasp why and how improper usage of land occurs.

The factors involved in land issues go far beyond the availability of modern agricultural equipment or seeds, or even redistribution of land parcels alone. Socioanthropological factors, such as migration, population pressure, land scarcity, and traditional farming practices, economic factors, such as urban–rural development and employment rates, and biophysical factors, such as climate, soil structure, nutrient availability, topography, and natural vegetation, all come into play. Though the richness of the interaction within God's creation is more than we sometimes want to imagine, if we are to be wise and caring cocreators in bringing to fruition the fullness of God's earth, then we are obliged to give prayerful attention to signs of the "whole creation's travail" (Rom. 8:22).

Because there are so many variables to consider, it may be easier to comprehend the "whys" and "hows" of land marginalization by focusing on a few examples. While looking at specific examples, we must keep in mind that approximately 70 percent of the world's people live in societies in which access to land for agricultural purposes means access to employment, food, and social respectability. Throughout Latin America, one of the primary factors contributing to the marginalization of land is the size of land holdings. In 1975, 7 percent of Latin America's land owners possessed 93 percent of the cultivable land. What, then, of the other 93 percent of the land owners? Of the remaining land available to them, only 7 percent was worth tilling, meaning that some were inevitably forced to farm land that was already less than productive and could easily become wholly useless. Even as we as individuals are equipped to perform some tasks better than other tasks, so different soil types and topographies are best suited for various purposes. Discovering the types and ranges of natural constraints and working within them is the art and science of husbandry—which by definition means: "the care of a household; judicious use of resources; conservation." In many parts of the world, the skill of husbandry is prevented from being practiced by socioeconomic structures that force the peasantry into food-cropping soils that are better suited for forest and that allow, if not encourage, large land owners to exploit the land for short-term profits rather than long-term sustenance.

When the issue of potential world famine has been raised in the past, people have ameliorated their concern by pointing to the large unused areas of land in the tropics, implying that possible cropland had yet to be tapped. There is good reason, however, why these lands have been left under forest or bush cover. In sub-Saharan Africa, much of the land is practically uncultivable due largely to the taxing climate, which results in a very precariously balanced ecosystem. Furthermore, the agricultural system of shifting cultivation and the political structure of a chiefship over people rather than land parcels have discouraged the notion of permanent individual rights to land.

In order to appreciate the interplay of environmental and human factors in tropical ecosystems, we should consider the example of Sierra Leone, a small West African coastal nation. The traditional system of agriculture practiced in many tropical environments is known as "slash and burn" or "bush-fallow farming," which has been viewed not so much as an act of savage ignorance as an appropriate response to the nature of the soil. The ancient farmer would clear land of full forest growth a month or so before the rainy season, allow the felled wood to dry, set it on fire to reduce the vegetation to ashes for soil enrichment, and then scatter-plant various crops in the ecologically sound manner of mixed-cropping. The plots would be cultivated until they failed to produce good yields due to nutrient depletion one to four years, after which time they were allowed to regenerate forest growth four to six years, while the farmer reenacted the process on other plots. Obviously such a system requires low population density and large amounts of farmable lands. As those conditions have increasingly been altered the period of fallow time has decreased in length (now one to three years). Land is overused, and farmers are forced to infringe upon forests, hillsides, and grassy regions, with disastrous consequences.

The land in Sierra Leone, as in other tropics, is characterized by virtually nonexistent topsoil, very shallow subsoil, and a hard crust beneath. Given such a tenuous base, promotion of soil cover cannot be overly stressed. An environmentally sound system of agriculture should allow the land to replenish itself with natural growth/fallow periods and should avoid taking the land out of its natural contour as much as possible. True "slash and burn" farming met those criteria by keeping the delicate African soils under the protective canopy of tree and bush growth, and thus protected from wind, sun, and heavy rain. Disturbance of the topsoil layers by plowing, use of heavy equipment, and wind or water erosion very quickly leads to infertility and desertification of the land in West Africa, as in other regions, including the United States. Furthermore, as tropical forests around the world are destroyed, the earth's largest and most important natural sink for CO_2 storage and usage is eradicated, promoting the "greenhouse" effect. Simply stated, the "greenhouse" effect is a buildup of CO_2 in our outer atmosphere that traps in the heat and thus contributes to a warming climatic change. Due to human actions that both cause and derive from our present environmental situation, not only is land being misused and permanently marginalized, but our global ecosystem is being jeopardized.

It is a well-documented statement in the science of ecology that "you can't do just one thing." Everything literally affects everything else in a natural system. In America today, for example, the petroleum crisis is more than an "energy" crunch in the usual sense of the word. Due to America's great dependence on oil for the manufacturing and usage of farm equipment, the production of fertilizers, herbicides, and pesticides and the maintenance of the farms themselves, our food production would be reduced by 50 percent if petroleum were removed from the picture. Having replaced manual labor with machines, our "agripower" capacity is such that less than 5 percent of America's population can feed the other 95-plus percent, but not without costs to our land's long-term capacity to produce and to the economy.

In developing countries, where people are much less dependent on chemicals and petroleum in farming, the system is much more labor-intensive. Knowing this, it is sobering to look at what is happening to the labor force as a result of recent rural–urban migration. The effects of rural–urban migration in Sierra Leone are particularly striking. The western area of Sierra Leone houses the country's capital of Freetown, built at the base of a mountainous peninsula that was once covered with tropical forest. Now the area has a population density of 907 people per square mile, and the remaining regions in the country average 72 people per square mile. While the barrios and squatter settlements that result from a vast rural–urban influx are not comfortable places to live in any nation, due to the multitude of social, economic, and health problems they present, in Sierra Leone, squatter settlements are particularly intolerable due to the area's geography. The incoming migrant, motivated by hopes of a better life, is generally unable to find housing in the overcrowded city itself, and so moves onto the 30° to 60° slopes surrounding the city. These new settlers, unable to secure full employment in town, inevitably brush a small patch of land for a garden, even though such action is illegal, merely to feed themselves. In 1975, the Ministry of Forestry initially denied what aerial photography indisputably revealed: that 42 percent of the peninsula was illegally under tillage, which in such mountainous conditions greatly increases the risk of major flooding and soil erosion. Unable to offer viable solutions to problems in the city and equally unable to offer significant help to rural areas, such as providing water, electricity, schools, and roads, the government does nothing.

Nearly 800 million people in the world live in absolute poverty. Though America's land is being marginalized through overuse and misuse, we have yet to feel keenly the inevitable consequences of our actions. But for those 800 million at the very margin of existence already, some of the further human and land marginalizing consequences of poor agricultural methods are: (1) watershed reduction, at a time when more water is needed by the population and would-be crops; (2) pollution of the available water due to overuse both up and down stream; (3) inability of the soil to hold water as its delicate surface is destroyed; (4) destruction of wildlife habitats such that small game, which once served as important dietary supplements, are driven out of the area, promoting malnutrition even as crop yields decline and risk of disease increases with overcrowding; (5) severe siltation of the estuaries and harbor during the rainy season due to tons of soil being washed from the hillsides in the high intensity rains, when over eighty inches of rain may fall in a period of two months; and (6) reduction of seafood sources due to the mineral-particulate pollution.

But this cycle of consequences need not continue. If we return to our original statement that it is the method of land use that determines the hospitality of the land, we regain the awareness that we are responsible for discovering and maintaining the inherent hospitality of the land. In many developing nations, such as Sierra Leone, the ancient forms of land use, including "slash and burn" farming, were appropriate given the constraints of the land; however, as the population and lifestyles of people on the land have changed, in most instances due to outside influences like colonization, accompanying changes in agricultural methods have not occurred. This is in part due to the fact that the needs of the small landholders or landless tenant farmers in less-developed nations have never received priority placement on research agendas. It is also due to the fact that there are very few scientists in the developing countries. A Kenyan scientist, Thomas Odiambo, has suggested that, "Apart from such constraints as inadequate credit, poorly developed marketing outlets and a weak transport infrastructure, perhaps the most serious limitation is the inadequate body of research scientists capable of grappling with the biological constraints related to increased and stable agricultural yields, and the grossly underfinanced agricultural research and development activities."

As highly techno-scientific as our nation is, we can still see the folly of proposing scientific answers alone to problems that we now recognize are interdisciplinary and complex. If we acknowledge education as a means to greater self-reliance, however, then we must consider scientific education as an essential factor in developing an indigenous capacity for agricultural innovations that can mitigate marginalization. When advocating self-reliance in less-developed countries, we must be certain that our motives are not really calling for the creation of closed systems that do not impinge upon our consciousness. For scientific endeavors, as all human endeavors, are able to advance only by building on foundations established by others, and therefore require that communication be constant among all those who are working on improved land management schemes.

Greater self-reliance is likewise required in America's land usage today if our land is to be maintained for good use tomorrow. Through not being in actual contact with our land, we Americans have developed an unrealistic perspective of it as something either to keep or to use up; or perhaps more commonly we do not think of it at all but have left it in the hands of corporations. In the economic scales used in America, there are countless examples of the little value that "human size" is accorded. It is not just in developing countries that farmers cannot afford to live in the rural areas anymore. In a 1970 *National Geographic* article, the author writes, "How many have given up can be seen in such figures as these: In 1910 our farm population accounted for a third of the U.S. total. By 1969 it was a mere twentieth. People leave rural areas at an average rate of six hundred and seventy thousand a year; to become added tinder for the riots that can be labelled one of the social consequences. . . ." And so the cycle can go on, with further marginalization of both human and land resources— unless we act on the privilege and responsibility of being cocreators with God to assure that God's hospitable creation, the earth, is maintained for future generations of God's children.

SELECTION A
IN PLYMOUTH COUNTY, IOWA, THE RICH TOPSOIL'S GOING FAST. ALAS.

by Curtis Harnack
from *The New York Times,* July 11, 1980.

In Iowa, June is a hopeful time; green burgeoning fields stretch to the horizon. During the week I spent on my ancestral farm, of which I still own a piece, I heard first-hand reports of a severe agricultural depression. Older neighbors recalled with foreboding the late 1920's, when farmers were the first to feel the Great Depression. The weather, usually the chief topic of conversation, had been replaced by concern over the economy.

And yet severe storms this spring caused damage perhaps ultimately more devastating than the present low price for corn. The United States Soil Conservation Service estimated that 4.3 million acres of Iowa land suffered the worst soil erosion in six years, with some acres losing 10 tons of topsoil because of heavy rains and poor planting practices.

My home county, Plymouth, in the northwest, was the worst hit. Row crops (primarily corn and soybeans) are extensively planted because they yield the best returns. Old-style crop rotation, alternating corn one year with oats the next, has been supplanted by heavy use of chemicals for weed and pest control, and fertilizer. Fields of small grain (oats and barley) used to stop water runoffs; alfalfa and grasses were sown for hay, but also because their root systems held the soil and replenished it.

These days a farmer eliminates even the fence rows if possible; every foot of land (worth $3,000 an acre before the current depression set in) must be used. Contour farming, which is widely followed, helps prevent erosion somewhat, but terraces and grass strips in waterways would be even more effective. A landowner farmer knows that wise husbandry is in his best interest, but with more and more tracts rented out, tenant farmers often seek the immediate production goal, with little regard for the long-range effects.

In 1877, William B. Close, a pioneer British settler in my home county, measured the topsoil and found it two to three feet deep. ''The subsoil extends in depth from fifteen to thirty feet and even more in some places that I have seen, then clay is reached. As if nature had not done enough in giving so rich a soil, it is provided with a splendid fertiliser in phosphates of lime, with which the soil is impregnated.'' A little over a century later, in June of this year, the Iowa State Conservationist, William Brunner, was quoted in *The Des Moines Register* as having said: ''Many of our sloping soils have only six inches of topsoil left in Iowa. And when you lose half an inch or more like happened in some of our fields in less than a month, it's serious.''

With the depletion of topsoil, chemical fertilizers become even more important in order to achieve high yields, but the cost further reduces the farmer's already lean margin of profit. Because of chemical farming, surface well water is largely unsafe. During my visit, tubular plastic water pipes were being laid below the frost line, linking my farm to a reliable source of clean water. The elaborate conduit system was described to me as an enterprise similar to rural electrification in the 1930's. No more worry about wells going dry. Towns have always had their bulbous water tanks high on stilts, the name emblazoned in six-foot letters. Now farmers have their own water tanks; I glimpsed one in the distance, six miles away. The water comes from limestone rock, underground streams that also feed the Great Lakes.

When I was a boy, the cool draughts of water gushed out of the pump spout after I had leaped a good deal upon the handle with all my weight. Our well was 40 feet deep, the water rather hard and full of minerals—healthy water, which my New York dentist years later claimed was responsible for my excellent teeth. This gift of the land is no longer there.

Few surface wells anywhere in my county are safe for drinking. When I first heard this, I thought bottled water might be the simplest solution: but, of course, I was forgetting the principal use of water on a farm—for the livestock. A single milch cow might drink 30 gallons a day. Contaminated water would result in milk that wouldn't test out; or the taint of nitrates might pass into the flesh of hogs and beef cattle, and eventually into humans.

Mr. Brunner, the State Conservationist, said: ''It can take 100 to 500 years to create an inch of topsoil that can wash away in a single heavy rainstorm.'' Iowa possessed some of the richest land in the world, but we let much of it blow away or run off, and have become addicted to potentially harmful chemicals in order to keep the crops coming.

In 100 years, the Iowa farmer has exploited and diminished his heritage of soil—a staggering spendthrift spree.

SELECTION B
ALARM HEARD ON SHRINKING U.S. FARMLAND
by David F. Salisbury
Reprinted from the *Christian Science Monitor,* July 23, 1980.

Every time you go through a checkout line at the supermarket on a weekly shopping trip, the equivalent of 60,000 acres of US farmland has been washed and blown away through erosion since your previous trip to the market.

Another 60,000 acres is converted into land for houses, shops, roads, power plants, coal mines, and other nonagricultural uses.

This loss of farmland, acceptable in the 1950s and '60s—a time of large crop surpluses and increasing yields per acre—is being viewed with alarm by agriculture experts.

"There are many political historians who believe the United States is on the verge of losing its pre-eminent position of world leadership—from lack of arms superiority, from lack of domestic energy resource alternatives, from lack of technology innovation," Charles E. Little, president of the American Land Forum, has observed. "Maybe one more 'lack' should be added to the list: the inability to protect the greatest body of farmland of any nation on the face of the earth."

In the past, mechanization, fertilizers, pesticides, and irrigation have enabled American farmers to replace land with water and energy. But now, "with the cost of energy skyrocketing, the depletion of soil and water resources [caused in part by the side effects of technology], and maybe even the climate turning against us, there is a serious question whether American agriculture can continue to 'replace' farmland losses through technology," a study by the National Association of Counties Research Foundation warns. "Evidence is mounting that it cannot: Per-acre yields from US croplands peaked in 1972 and have since then fluctuated rather widely at lower levels."

Those who have studied the situation largely agree that the nation has reached a point where each acre of prime farmland that is developed for other purposes—such as shopping centers, housing, industrial parks, and so on—threatens a permanent loss in total US agricultural capacity.

The ultimate implications of this situation appear quite serious. US agricultural exports are expected to top $38 billion this year, about 20 percent of the nation's total exports. These farm exports are extremely important in offsetting the money paid out for oil imports. A reduction in agricultural production would result in greater inflationary pressures on groceries. It could also weaken the US dollar and thereby increase the price of imported goods.

David L. Brown, a sociologist with the Economics, Statistics, and Cooperative Service, estimates that the best farmland is being converted to urban uses at twice the rate of poorer land.

Since the poor land is more easily eroded, the amount of soil blowing away or flowing down US rivers could increas.. John F. Timmons, an agricultural economist at Iowa State University, predicts a 72 percent increase in soil erosion through 1985 in the Corn Belt, partly as a result of this trend to poorer land.

Already, some 100 million acres of farmland in the US have been ruined by erosion. Much of this total was lost in the dust bowl of the 1930s. This experience led to adoption of extensive soil conservation practices. But experts have been warning that economic pressures stemming from rising land prices and the end of large agricultural surpluses have led to a relaxation in soil protection measures.

"Of course, this situation cannot continue without impairing the cropland's ability to produce. Either large public and private investments must be made in erosion control improvements and practices or less erodable land must be retained within the cropland base . . . ," Professor Timmons argues.

The price of agricultural land has been increasing at a rate 2½ times that of inflation.

One result, notes Mr. Little, is that "farmland is in the process of being priced out of the market for farm use."

This reality is the genesis of the adage "Scratch a farmer and you find a developer."

No longer is the opportunity to subdivide farmland into housing lots limited to the fringes of large cities. A US Department of Agriculture analysis of census statistics has disclosed that the long-term trend of population migration from country to city has reversed.

"Increasingly, rural America is scarcely distinguishable from suburban America," Mr. Little observes.

The result is that more family farmers, like the Carlsons of Northglenn, Colo., sell their land for housing or even develop it themselves into housing tracts. In 1961 the Carlsons decided that "houses were a better crop" than the wheat and alfalfa they had been growing.

Besides tempting farmers out of agriculture, high land prices also make it difficult, if not impossible, for city dwellers to "return to the land" and farm profitably.

Still, most Americans do not relate the conversion of farmland to other uses with the supply and price of food, says Richard C. Collins of the University of Virginia.

Only two federal agencies, the Agriculture Department and the Environmental Protection Agency, take this factor into account in their planning. Increasingly, states have begun enacting various farmland protection programs. But in general these have not been the highly agricultural states.

Such programs entail some form of land-use planning, a concept that has been opposed by farmers who view this as government intrusion on their right to do what they wish with their land. In February farm lobbyists were instrumental in defeating a House bill to authorize studying the problem.

Session 8

TECHNOLOGY

Bible Study and Discussion

Ecclesiasticus 17:1–32
I Corinthians 3:10–17

- Read and discuss the Biblical passages.
- Compare the passage from Ecclesiasticus with your discussion of the Creation Narrative (Genesis 1:1–2:4) in Session 6. Are there differences in the view of the Creator and the creation?
- You may want to extend your study by including Ecclesiasticus 18:1–29.
- Reflect on the passage from I Corinthians, especially 3:12–13. What message does it hold for the contemporary Christian?

Moving Along

- After reading the essay "Technology" (pp. 102–110), define and discuss the terms: infrastructure, appropriate technology, labor-intensive, capital-intensive, and agribusiness.
- Read Selection A (pp. 111–113). What are the moral and ethical implications of "risk–benefit analysis"?
- After reading Selections B and C (pp. 113–118), discuss the statement: Technology is both the problem and the answer.

Preparing for the Next Session

- Identify a moderator for the next discussion session.
- Call attention to the readings for Session 9, pages 000–000.
- Ask the participants to prepare prayers for use at the next meeting.
- If you did not cover all the issues in this session, negotiate with the group for additional time.
- Have you considered asking a resource person to join your group?

Ending

- Read aloud:
  Genesis 11:1–9
- Pause for silent meditation and reflection.
- Share prayers prepared by participants.
- The moderator reads aloud:

> Whatever befalls the earth befalls the people of the earth. Humans did not weave the web of life, we are merely stranded in it. Whatever we do to the web we do to ourselves . . . tribe follows tribe and nation follows nation like the waves of the sea. It is the order of nature and regret is useless. Your time of decay may be distant, but it will surely come, for even the whites whose God walked and talked with them as friend to friend, cannot be exempt from the common destiny. We may be family after all. We will see.
>
> Chief Sealth (Seattle), 1855

- Pause for silent meditation and reflection.
- Read aloud:

> *For stewardship of creation*
>
> O merciful Creator, your hand is open wide to satisfy the needs of every living creature: Make us always thankful for your loving providence; and grant that we, remembering the account that we must one day give, may be faithful stewards of your good gifts; through Jesus Christ our Lord, who with you and the Holy Spirit lives and reigns, one God, for ever and ever.

And at the Very End

Have the group assess the learning they have gained in the session.
- What did you learn?
- Identify any new insights you gained.
- What issues discussed in the session would you like to know more about?

Technology

Central to the subject of agrarian reform, both in developed and developing countries, is the topic of technology; for in many ways the application of yet another technology has been a mode of trying to escape agrarian "reform" in its strictest sense. Technological innovations have greatly altered farming in the United States, with far-reaching consequences for America's entire social structure and physical environment as well as for its role in the international world. The introduction of modern technology in the less-developed nations has been even more revolutionary due to the technology's foreign origins and the consequent lack of continuity between it and the social structures into which it is placed. A now famous article, entitled "Steel Axes for Stone-Age Australians," discusses some of the issues that arise when a technology is interjected into a social, political, and economic system that has not been designed to support or use it. This essay has a similar purpose. It will review trends in agricultural technologies per se; but more importantly, it will consider their effect on the quality of life.

A list of the technologies currently in use in American farming includes: herbicides, pesticides, and fertilizers, high-yield variety grains, genetic manipulation of germ plasm for hybrid seeds, managerial, accounting, and civil engineering skills, extension programs, various cropping patterns, irrigation schemes, combine-harvesters, seed drills, tractors, and others. This very abbreviated list of widely applied agricultural technologies suggests that today's farming community is highly conversant with the scientific, business, and industrial sectors, which is indeed the case. In fact, the American farming community in the traditional sense has been largely replaced by the industrialized agricultural sector. An historical view of the industrialization of Western agriculture will not only help us to understand how we arrived at our present state of farming as agribusiness, but also how the spread of agricultural technology will influence developing countries.

The development of industrial technology in nineteenth-century Europe was the beginning of the trend we have now completed: that of moving from a decentralized rural population to an urban population with more centralized control. A key element in industrial societies is the distinction between the designer/decision-maker and the majority, who operate machines without much share in the planning. On the one hand, as Guy Hunter points out in *Modernizing Peasant Societies: A Comparative Study in Asia and Africa,* "(this) makes possible the success and scale of industry by multiplying the effect of designing and managerial skill through the employment of a huge operative labour force." On the other hand, it diminishes the self-reliance of the labor force, making them susceptible to layoffs and market fluctuations.

As the basic motivation of industry is to produce goods for a market for profit, the insurance of markets becomes critical. In a predominantly farming society, however, a lack of purchasing power can often exist; therefore, in nineteenth-century Europe, "the modernization of agricultural production and management became essential [to industry]" (Hunter, *Modernizing Peasant Societies*). This modernization process was slowly accomplished; first, "by separation from communal to individual land holdings; by adding complexity to crops and rotations; by bringing in mechanical power and the design and maintenance contracts from the industrial sector; by scientific plant genetics; and, almost last of all, by the elaboration of chemical fertilization and control." (Hunter, *Modernizing Peasant Societies*) Only in this very last stage of heavy dependence on the petrochemical industry did management specialization become possible and necessary through the increased contact of farmers with industry and the need, therefore, for the farmers to adopt industrial concepts such as cost accounting. As Guy Hunter further states: "Agriculture, then, in its heavy capital-intensive structure, business management and use of factory techniques, begins to look more and more like industry." Conversely, industry begins to look more and more like the new agriculture; and as the world population burgeons, industry can be assured that a market for food will be expanding. In Revelation it was prophesied that "a piece of bread could buy a bag of gold." This situation is no longer so distantly prophetic!

A comprehensive evaluation of the human and ecological consequences of the comparatively recent technological revolution in farming is only beginning to emerge; however, topical critiques have been offered throughout the past twenty years. By piecing together some of those separate observations, an overview of the total impact of technology on agricultural systems may be gained.

Social Systems

One of the immediate social consequences of the use of modern technology has been the development of an entrepreneur and/or foreman role in farming communities, which were originally more homogeneous. An account from Tunisia expresses a common social evolution abruptly brought about through the introduction of farm machinery:

> . . . machinery became a factor of production separable from land and households . . . a new role appeared as some people

purchased tractors and combines to rent to others . . . The introduction of machinery in agriculture has modified work patterns.
A combine, for instance, requires five to six men in addition to
those who use tractors to haul the grain wagons to the storehouse.
The work rhythm of all these men is set by the man who owns
the machine . . . In the place of the old semi-independent sharecroppers, sharing the product under a system of devolution of
responsibility, there are now work gangs tied to the rhythm and
productivity of the tractor, the combine and the diesel pump.
Workers are paid for their time, and the close supervision required to ensure that the requisite amount of work is done has
contributed to the emergence of a foreman role. Control through
supervision or through wages has become a necessary ingredient
of the social system . . . The machinery that allows the farmers
and cooperative leaders to control their workers also involves
them in a new network of obligations toward the control structure of the national society. Mechanized agriculture is market-
oriented, and thus there is a dependency on the market, the road
system, the telephone, and the centralized banking system which
supplies the credit to purchase and maintain the equipment.
. . . Mechanization is usually advocated for economic reasons
such as increased productivity; yet it is clear that there are political and social consequences as well, both at the local level and
in the area of local, national relations. In thinking about agricultural change, these factors should be considered as well. (Nicholas S. Hopkins, "Modern Agriculture and Political Centraliza-
tion: A Case from Tunisia," *Human Organization,* 37(1):83–
87.)

In America, with our extreme condition of international dependence, to the extent that oil under the earth thousands of miles away
from our shores is considered to be "our national interest," we may
well ask why dependency-creating factors ought to be considered in
planning agricultural change. Our industrialized agricultural system
has taken us so far away from self-sufficiency that we may fail at
times to even recognize it as a primary value upon which our nation
was founded. In sharing our technological know-how with developing
nations, we must ask ourselves, "What are we trying to do?" A pin
distributed by the Information Center on Instructional Technology in
Washington, D.C., humorously points out the zeal with which we go
about giving "stone-age Australians" steel axes: "Technology is the
answer!—but what is the question?"

Perhaps the most far-reaching agricultural technology mission to developing countries that has been undertaken to date is the Green Revolution. Begun in the 1960s, the Green Revolution can be briefly de-

fined as a phenomenon characterized by a rapid growth in grain yields resulting from the introduction of a "package" of technological inputs, which include high-yielding grain varieties (HYVs), heavy petrochemical fertilization, pesticides, and irrigation schemes. Ostensibly, one of the goals of development projects is to increase self-reliance within nations; however, the above technological inputs and the technical skills to make use of the sensitive HYVs are generally not available in developing countries. Moreover, the societal infrastructure required to support such technologies, for example, by distributing seeds and chemicals or marketing harvested grains on a large scale, does not exist in developing countries. Technological planners have all too often assumed that regions adopting HYVs can, and will, follow the model of infrastructure operating in developed nations; however, such has not been the case.

Lester Brown has stated in "The Social Impact of the Green Revolution" (*International Conciliation,* 581) that "All technological innovation leads to some social change and disruption. What is different about the introduction of the new seeds is the quantum jump in technology they represent." What is only recently becoming realized is that the modern technologies may also represent quantum leaps in social disruption. Perhaps this recognition will yet be in time to ameliorate social upheavals and allow a new path for development to arise.

The World Bank's science and technology adviser, Charles Weiss, Jr., wrote in the March 16, 1979 issue of *Science:*

> Twenty years ago there were few who doubted that technological progress—then conceived as powered by advances in science and engineering in the developed countries—would lead to a better world. The world was then confident that the technology needed by the developing countries was available to them, perhaps with *minor* modifications, in the developing countries and that the major problem of technology policy in developing countries was to master that technology and to overcome cultural and institutional obstacles to its rapid acceptance. Today this automatic acceptance of technological change is questioned in both developed and developing countries—not because of any generalized loss of faith in technology, but because of greater understanding, born of experience, that the impact of a technology depends on the institutional, economic, social and ecological situation into which it is introduced; and conversely, that government policies, market incentives, and institutional and social constraints may have as much influence on the evolution of technology as the activities of formal technological institutions. . . . This . . . has led [tech-

nological] policy-makers to recognize the need for more *appropriate technology; . . .* technology that is smaller in scale, more labor-intensive, more subject to local mastery, repair, and control, and more in ecological and cultural harmony with its surroundings than the technology that would be likely to be used in an analogous situation in the North.

Charles Weiss, Jr. refers to the above perspective on technology as "holistic technology assessment" and one that "demands a long time horizon, a willingness to disaggregate, and an attention to economic, technological, cultural and sociological detail." While such a policy has yet to be implemented effectively, it is definitely a step in the right direction. In the past, the many agricultural-scheme failures that were suffered and the sense of hopelessness that these failures generated stemmed from the fact that attention was focused on the "final situation as it could be," as opposed to an understanding of the existing farm system and a consideration of new solutions. If personal and cultural self-determination and integrity are to be upheld in our use of technology, not only must the temptation to go directly from A to Z be resisted, but also the assumption must not be made that every society's evolution is the same; the new path of development now being tread very likely does not lead to Z. Examination of some of the ecological consequences of the previous prevalent technologies tends to lead to an overall conclusion that more appropriate technologies are urgently required in the developed and developing countries alike.

Natural Systems

A brief review of some of the technologies listed at the beginning of this essay reveals that although we are the only species on earth that utilizes technology, there are other powers on earth beyond our control.

Of the agricultural technologies listed, the tractor is one of the most widely used. Because of its effectiveness in many respects, and the ease with which it can be exported, the tractor is often used as an item in foreign aid, though it is notoriously uneconomic and damaging to the delicate topsoils when introduced into many small-scale tropical farming situations. Wendell Berry, in *The Unsettling of America,* makes an effective case against the use of some of the heavier tractor equipment in temperate climates as well, due to the serious ill-effects of tamping down the soil and destroying the crumb-structure so that its fertility is reduced. Because of its widespread usage and general acceptance as a benign piece of machinery, the tractor is sometimes overlooked as the truly revolutionary item of technology it is. In most instances, the introduction of the tractor means the withdrawal of draft animals from the scene, which means the removal not only of a self-renewing source of traction, but also of a producer of milk, dung, for use as fertilizer or fuel, and, eventually, hides, horn, bonemeal, or even food. The loss of a natural source of fertilizer means that some other source for soil enrichment becomes necessary. This need is filled today by chemical fertilizers, which might best be considered in the context of a "package deal" of new seed varieties, pesticides, herbicides, and fertilizers, as this is the commonest way these technologies are introduced today.

Since the inception of agriculture as a science, plant breeders have been developing "new and better" varieties of plants, even as a natural-selection process of breeding is constantly occurring in the wild. The basis for both the natural and scientific production of new varieties of crops is the great diversity of species and subspecies in nature that can interbreed. As Pat Mooney states in "The Seeds of Disaster," "The more different species there are of any given crop the more chance there is that there will be enough of them capable of resisting a particular disease. And since the diseases and pests are constantly mutating into more diverse forms, we need plants capable of making similar steady changes."

This biological fact is the basis of the notion of "survival of the fittest" in the process of evolution of successful species through natural selection. It is also the core concept in the development of the high-yield variety grains used in the Green Revolution and other specially bred seeds. Two severe dangers have arisen through the overbreeding of plants: (1) genetically highly uniform crops are being grown that are delightfully uniform in their response to fertilizer and irrigation, but that are also uniformly vulnerable to attack from specialized predators; and (2) the genetic pools of entire species are becoming extinct in certain areas and even globally as resistant strains are sent throughout the world that are only resistant until a new predator arises, at which time whole species can disappear. The unfortunate result is a decrease in the diversity of plant life on earth.

Disastrous examples of the dangers of overhybridization and uniformity in plant species have occurred frequently: In 1956, in California, the alfalfa crop was devastated by aphids; in 1967, in England, there was not a single commercial wheat that was resistant to rust; in

1970, in the Southern United States, a corn blight hit, destroying half the crop; and in India, in 1971, the pearl millet crop was wiped out by a downy mildew against which there were no resistant strains; starvation ensued for thousands. Because of the creation of these "pure" strains which basically cannot fend for themselves as they have had all the variability bred out of them, a constant battle is being waged in which the research scientists are endeavoring to keep one jump ahead of predatory diseases and crop pests. It is usually more than the scientists can do, and entire crops fail due to the specialized frailty of the hybrid plants.

While the remaining small farmers do not fare well under these conditions, the agrochemical companies flourish; for aside from owning many of the seed companies in the world today, they possess the pesticides, herbicides, and fertilizers that are essential for plant protection. Though Rachel Carson's books *The Silent Spring* and *Since Silent Spring* helped call attention to the large-scale use of synthetic broad-spectrum pesticides, these continue to be used today in increasing quantities. While many of the insecticides and pesticides are of great value in protecting crops and livestock from predator attack due to their persistent residual and nonspecific toxic action, it is this very quality that makes them a human health hazard due to the buildup of residue on and in the plants. Furthermore, their nonspecific action makes them poisonous for small animals in general and insects that are beneficial for crops, such as ladybugs. The problem of pesticides is further complicated since those pests that do survive become resistant to biocidal agents and cause more destruction than they originally did.

Prior to the advent of biocides as a prevalent technology, the science of food toxicity was not particularly important. Today, however, the addition of chemicals to our food before it is even harvested or processed is a serious matter. Some of the chemicals used as pesticides and herbicides have later been proven to have phytotoxic properties, that is, they are poisonous to the plant itself. The problem is exacerbated by the occurrence of insecticide residue on animal feeds, which then are stored and concentrated in the meat and milk and ultimately are ingested by man, often at high toxicity levels. Every American alive today is thought to carry measurable quantities of DDT in his/her body fat compartment with plateaus of 10 ppm; and while no alarmingly deleterious effects have been recorded, foreign chemicals in the body can certainly not be advantageous.

Alternatives to the technologies presently in use in agribusiness do exist, and more are being developed. The value of traditional intercultivation of annual crops has been recognized anew as having a soil-fertility maintenance effect; biological control of insect pests—the introduction of natural-enemy insects to prey on those insects that are pests to the crops—is being given more research attention; and a multitude of appropriate mechanical technologies, which are labor-intensive and energy-saving, are being considered by inventive minds around the world. Peddle-power threshers, row weeders, and better hand plows are being developed by indigenous farmers with the help of specially trained extension agents. In many places in West Africa, the possibilities of intensively cultivating inland swamps, which prior to now have not been farmed, are being explored with demonstration projects run by the peasant farmers themselves; and elsewhere, attempts to maximize the advantages of traditional working patterns, such as the working of community lands, are being tried with the aid of agricultural extension personnel.

Initial evaluations of modern technologies primarily tended to consider the economic factors involved in modern industrialized agribusiness, or the degree to which the technologies were successful in making developing countries conform to developed countries. In both instances, efficiency in the short term was a prime interest. Articles tended to be entitled "Miracle or Mirage" or other such "either-or" options, and technology as a whole was either lauded or condemned. In 1980, most critics of today's agricultural–technological systems do not advocate a complete abandonment of mechanized and scientific technology, nor do they suggest that we redouble our efforts of the past, for there have been some gross errors and dangerous trends. As Wendell Berry wrote in *The Unsettling of America:* ". . . Rather a picking and choosing of techniques and tools to get the job done in the most energy conserving way possible" is the sound advice that must be increasingly heeded. Diversity in natural systems promotes stability and provides insurance against calamity, and the same is true in social systems and technologies. A combination of scientific understanding and achievements with a sensitivity to traditional infrastructures and local conditions is likely to produce an appropriate technology for the future—if we are willing to make that combination.

SELECTION A

HAZARDOUS WASTES: GHOSTS OF A PRODIGAL PAST

by Paul Langner

Reprinted from Technology Review, August/September, 1980.

They reaped their harvests and left—the Monsantos, the Merrimacs, the Stepans, the Stauffers—chemical companies that for more than 100 years had kept North Woburn, Mass. busy and prosperous with industrial activity, making such products as glue, pesticides, and explosives.

They left behind tons of decaying hides and as-yet-unknown quantities of heavy metals and other pollutants, including hexavalent chromium and arsenic, a known carcinogen. Most of the land where their buildings once stood, about 120 acres, is now barren, a ruin of weathered foundations and a lone smokestack.

Less than a mile downwind in a neighborhood called Walnut Hill, the residents await October, when the Massachusetts Department of Public Health (DPH) has promised the results of a study to learn whether the unusually high rate of cancer in Woburn is associated with the wastes in the former industrial, site. In 10 years, according to DPH statistics, Woburn should have had 503 cancer cases. It had 569, a 13 percent excess. Among them are 14 leukemia cases, 8 within a half-mile radius of one another.

For two weeks in June and July, interviewers from the DPH and the U.S. Center for Disease Control in Atlanta interviewed the parents of leukemic children and friends and relatives of 50 deceased Woburn cancer victims to determine whether there is a pattern of morbidity. But the residents suspect what epidemiologists already know—that it will be very difficult to link the respository of hazardous wastes with any pattern of illness revealed by the study.

Woburn is not Love Canal, where the chemical wastes dumped by the Hooker Chemical Co. in the 1940s are now seeping into cellars and oozing to the surface, and residents have experienced an abnormally high incidence of birth defects and other ills.

In Woburn, however, neither the wastes nor their links, if any, to the ills of the residents are so obvious or dramatic. Because the connection is so tenuous, Woburn is apt to become a paradigm for the toxic-waste problem that, in the last three or four years, has moved toward the center of national consciousness. There are thousands of abandoned waste dumps across the nation, most of them near or even within populous cities and towns, and we are only beginning to evaluate the hazards they may represent.

The Disinherited

The dumps are orphans, deposited on the public's doorstep by industries that out of ignorance, sloth, or financial necessity failed to dispose of their wastes properly. Ironically, despite the wealth generated by more than a century of exuberant industrial activity, the public seems unable to find the resources necessary to understand and deal with the residue.

The Massachusetts Department of Environmental Quality Engineering (DEQE) has had to scrounge for funds to perform even simple tests on the Woburn arsenic and chromium pits. And when Richard Leighton, an engineer with DEQE, tried to put up a fence to keep unsuspecting people out of the area, he was able to raise only $200—enough to buy a roll of single-strand barbed wire. With the help of some juvenile offenders in a work-release program, he strung the wire himself.

William D'Annolfo, a real-estate developer who with some partners bought the Woburn land in 1968 for development as an industrial park, has now run up against a seemingly intractable problem. Every time he puts a backhoe or a bulldozer to work, he unearths piles of rotting hides that send hydrogen sulfide odors—the familiar rotten-egg smell—into Woburn and neighboring Reading. Cleaning the arsenic pits and chromium lagoons seems beyond his resources. Just to do an engineering study, he says, will cost him $100,000. According to one independent estimate, the cost of safely removing the arsenic and chromium and trucking it to a disposal facility would come to $6 million. D'Annolfo has said he might just walk away from his land if the price of cleaning it up turns out to be too high. The poisoned land would then revert to the city of Woburn, an orphan once more.

Dragon's Teeth

According to the U.S. Environmental Protection Agency, cleaning up all the known and suspected abandoned hazardous waste dumps in the nation could cost as much as $54 billion, a sum that no public agency is likely to raise. And industry does not consider itself liable. When manufacturers dumped their toxic wastes, no law forbade them to do it, and it is possible that much of the dumping was done in innocence by those who did not know they were sowing dragons' teeth. But in the case of Woburn, complaints date back to the 1860s, although apparently they had little effect.

Even today, Congress is running into heavy lobbying from the chemical industries as it debates a so-called "superfund" bill that would impose a tax on industrial products to provide about $1.9 billion toward cleaning up the wastes.

And just as environmentalism is practically a religion, industry often preaches the rival faith of risk-benefit analysis. But an increasingly suspicious and hostile public may force industry to change its attitudes. "Spare me your risk-benefit analysis," said one Woburn resident when the subject was raised at a recent public meeting. It would seem that for the affected community, the concept carries little moral or political clout.

As suggested in these pages by Nicholas Ashford [*"The Limits of Cost-Benefit Analysis in Regulatory Decisions," May 1980, p. 70*], benefits are difficult to measure in economic terms. They may include such things as better health and an improved environment, "but they defy accurate estimation and their recipients are not a well-organized lobbying group." To which Anne Anderson of Woburn would emphatically say, "Amen."

For years she had been telling her clergyman, the Rev. Bruce Young, rector of Trinity Episcopal Church, that she suspected something in the water had made her son ill with leukemia. Rev. Young was skeptical at first, even when she told him of other leukemia casès in his parish and nearby. Only when Woburn police, responding to an anonymous tip in May 1979, found 183 barrels of solvents dumped illegally in the new Woburn industrial park did things begin to happen.

SELECTION B
U.S. LACKS SYSTEM TO DETECT CHEMICAL CONTAMINANTS IN FOOD, AGENCY REPORTS
by Bryce Nelson
Reprinted from the Los Angeles Times, December 16, 1979

The United States has no system to detect most of the toxic chemicals that enter the nation's food supply—even though the technology for such detection exists, a federal agency reported Saturday.

The Office of Technology Assessment said major chemical contaminants of food in recent years were identified only after actual poisoning of animals or humans.

The agency said in a report that it found 243 incidents of chemical contamination of food in the United States in the decade from 1968 through 1978 that were serious enough to require governmental regulatory action—and these incidents were "just the tip of the iceberg," according to Catherine E. Woteki, the report's principal author. Many other incidents have escaped public notice, according to the report.

The reported incidents involved just about every kind of food and every region of the country.

The study was requested by the House Interstate and Foreign Commerce Committee because of concern over a number of food contamination incidents. They included the dumping of kepone in the James River in Virginia and PCB (polychlorinated biphenyls) contamination of food in Western states last summer, an incident that began in a Billings, Mont., packing plant.

Rep. Bob Eckhardt (D-Tex.), chairman of the Commerce Committee's oversight and investigations subcommittee, said the report "underscores the need for an immediate federal review of our ability to control harmful substances."

Eckhardt also said protecting the nation's food supply from chemical contaminants is one of the biggest environmental problems demanding immediate government attention.

The report said part of the reason for what has been a sketchy federal response to the problem so far is that "Congress has never directly addressed the environmental contamination of food."

Responsibility for toxic chemicals in food is now split among three federal agencies—the Food and Drug Administration, the Department of Agriculture and the Environmental Protection Agency.

"This problem deserves a good thorough look by Congress in its own right, rather than trying to (deal with) it with portions of existing law and procedures," said Joyce C. Lashof, the Office of Technology Assessment's assistant director for health and life sciences.

The office is an advisory arm of Congress that was created to provide expert scientific and technical studies for the lawmakers.

The report on "Environmental Contaminants in Food," which office director John H. Gibbons called "the first comprehensive examination of the problem," contained these findings:

- All of the major food contamination incidents the office studied were "marked by confusion." The report attributed this to fragmentation of federal authority and poor communication between state and federal agencies.
- When people or animals are stricken, it usually takes a long time to identify the chemical causing the contamination. And once the chemical is identified, it usually takes government agencies a long time to take regulatory action.
- There is no adequate federal program to assist state agencies responsible for chemical food contamination and most states do not have adequate programs of their own.
- Many states have reported contamination problems in recent years. California, for example, reported four chemical food contamination incidents during the decade studied, three caused by mercury and one by pesticides. The California incidents affected several categories of food—fruits and vegetables, fish and shellfish and meat and poultry.
- The present federal system is not designed to detect new toxic chemicals coming into the food supply, only those that have caused trouble in the past.
- Nearly all U.S. residents have low but detectable residues of some toxic environmental contaminants in their bodies. Not all of these residues, however, are from food.
- The cost of food and food animals destroyed because of chemical contamination in the 1968–1978 period has been placed a $282 million, but this figure is a "gross underestimation."
- Many reports of chemical contamination of food are made each year, but the office found no significant incidence of poisoning of food by radioactivity during the decade.

Although the federal government now monitors food for residues of pesticides, antibiotics, drugs and certain other chemical contaminants, it does not survey most of the thousands of toxic chemicals in the environment.

According to the report, the nation's regulatory monitoring system has failed to detect such environmental contaminants as PBBs (polybrominated biphenyls), PCBs and mercury as they have entered the food supply.

Despite chemical contamination of U.S. food, there have been no mass poisonings such as those in Japan where "foods contaminated with substances such as PCBs, mercury and cadmium have produced human illness and death," the report said.

Detection of new toxic chemicals entering the food supply is possible. Woteki said, through the use of "analytic chemical techniques, highly sophisti-cated instruments and computers which can determine patterns."

She said such techniques were used at three institutions—the University of New Orleans, the Virginia Institute of Marine Science and Michigan State University.

The Office of Technology Assessment does not make recommendations to Congress in its reports, but it did list "options" for the lawmakers to consider to remedy defects it found. These included:

- Improvement of the federal response to contamination incidents by desig-nation of a primary agency in the field, probably the FDA, and by the establishment of a federal center to collect and analyze toxic substances data similar to the Center for Disease Control in Atlanta.
- Establishment of "a national investigatory monitoring system that monitors for either suspected or uncharacterized environmental contaminants." The report said that with such a system, kepone might have been detected years earlier in Virginia's James River.

SELECTION C
THE SEEDS OF DISASTER
Reprinted from The *New Internationalist,* # 81, November, 1979.

Future world harvests are in grave danger. The problem is 'genetic erosion'; a phenomenon which biologists have worried about for years but about which the public seems to be virtually unaware. Biologist George M. Woodwell describes it as 'one of the great issues of our time, right up there with nuclear proliferation. The ultimate resource is the biota—there is no other. And we are destroying this resource.'

What is being 'eroded' is the genetic diversity of the world's crops. The more different species there are of any given crop the more chance there is that there will be enough of them capable of resisting a particular disease. And since the diseases and pests are constantly 'mutating' into more diverse forms, we need plants capable of making similar steady changes.

But the centralized development and high-pressure marketing of the new hybrid high-yielding varieties of seed are now spreading uniformity around the world and thus destroying the broad genetic base that has protected us for centuries. Whereas farmers used to save seeds from the previous year's har-vest to plant again, they cannot do that with the hybrids because they will not reproduce themselves correctly. Farmers now sell all their crop and have to go back to the seed companies for more.

Where do the old varieties go? Many are just lost forever—disappearing perhaps in the last bowl of porridge—but some others are being kept in gene banks, both public and corporate. United Brands controls two-thirds of the banana genetic material now in storage and there are similar collections of other crops. As Dr Margary Lee Oldfield recently wrote, those who controlled the world's remaining gene material in any crop 'would indeed possess almost infinite political and economic power'.

For the developing countries the irony is that they already 'own' much of the world's precious genetic diversity. But that source is now being raided by Western companies and then sold back to the Third World in the form of uniform and therefore vulnerable hybrids.

Warnings about the vulnerability of the new hybrids have been sounded at least since World War II, but no-one listened until blight struck the US corn crop in 1970, leaving the Southern states with only half a harvest. Dr William Caldwell of the US Department of Agriculture commented: 'We were sitting around fat, dumb and happy . . . the hybrids were doing well, and all of a sudden the disease hit. We didn't believe it could happen but it did.' What happened was that a disease had attacked the Texas (T) Cytoplasm which is common to almost all hybrids growing in the South. The proliferation of corporate brand names had disguised the fundamental genetic uniformity of the seeds. Frustrated and angry farmers have had several companies in the law courts ever since.

A year later in India the 'pearl millet' crop was devastated. It was a high-yielding but also highly uniform hybrid and when attacked by a form of downy mildew it was defenceless. At a symposium in 1977, Dr K.M. Saufeeulla of Mysore pointed out the difference between the two events. The US corn blight, he said, 'had led to an upward movement of prices'; the pearl millet wipeout in India 'led to starvation'.

Prompted by the corn blight a report by the US Academy of Sciences came to the conclusion that the US is 'impressively uniform genetically and impressively vulnerable'. The US millet crop, for example, consists of just three varieties and 75 per cent of Canadian bread wheat comes from four varieties. Similar disturbing figures can be produced for other North American and Australian crops.

When the West gets into trouble it looks to the Third World. University of California agronomist J. B. Kendrick recently calculated that, without regular infusion of germ plasm from the Third World, North Americans would soon experience devastating crop epidemics 'at a rapidly accelerating rate across the entire crop spectrum'.

In the 1970s, US pea and spinach producers narrowly escaped crop wipeouts by using emergency germ plasm introduced from India and Iran. And just a few years ago North African germ plasm rescued the Canadian oat crop from rust.

But now the Green Revolution and the whole 'genetics supply industry' are bringing about the rapid destruction of these centres of genetic diversity. The Cilician Plain in Turkey—once home to thousands of flax varieties—now grows only one imported variety. The Central Asian farmers who were the first to breed barley, now plant varieties imported from Sweden. Mexico's maize farmers—who virtually invented the crop—now buy hybrid maize seed from Pioneer Hi-bred International in the USA. FAO officials now predict that Middle East wheat may completely disappear by the end of the 1980s.

The replacement of these diverse crops by the Uniform Green Revolution hybrids is a result of market-place logic. If farmers were offered a high-yielding variety and could afford to pay for the massive inputs of fertilizer and irrigation they required, naturally they would take the opportunity. The country's genetic heritage was not of primary concern to either buyer or seller.

Originally financed by foundations such as Ford and Rockefeller, the Green Revolution very quickly involved the world's agrichemical companies who soon became the important salesmen. They reasonably saw it as an important marketing opportunity for their products. In some countries (Indonesia, for example) the Green Revolution was entirely sub-contracted to European chemical companies.

Originally they were primarily interested in the fertilizers and pesticides since these could be patented and sold for a high price. Seeds had always presented a problem because, however uniform the species, no two plants can ever be exactly the same and therefore cannot be strictly protected by patents.

To get round this, a new concept was introduced: 'Plant Breeders Rights' (PBR), which allows something closely equivalent to patent control over living organisms. In 1961, the principle of such rights was enshrined in a new international convention—the Union for the Protection of New Varieties of Plants, now linked with the UN system. Each year new countries are added to the list of those who honour these rights.

The effect on the seed industry was dramatic—small seed companies suddenly became important properties. Europe was quickest off the mark. In the week that PBR legislation was passed in the United Kingdom, one food and chemical corporation, Rank Hovis McDougall, bought out 84 small companies. And acquisitions were so extensive following the Plant Variety Act in the USA that the American Seed Trade Association devoted half its general meeting to a special symposium called 'How to Sell Your Seed Company'.

Who were the buyers? To no-one's very great surprise they turned out to be mainly the chemical giants. Today the seed industry is dominated by the likes of Ciba-Geigy, Sandoz, Pfizer, Upjohn, Monsanto, Union Carbide and Royal Dutch Shell. With the advent of PBR the seed industry was transformed from a host of small private enterprises into a chemical oligopoly.

Why were the seed producers bought by the chemical companies rather than by the grain or the farm machinery companies? The answer is that the chemical companies were already closely involved and they saw the chance of greater control. There was now the opportunity to dovetail their chemical and seeds research in such a way that one needs the other and the product of both can be sold together.

Suppose, for example, that a new high-yield variety of rice blows over in a high wind. The plant breeder has a choice of two remedies—either to breed a shorter stem or to breed a stronger stem. But of these two remedies the plant breeder who is also selling herb herbicides will be tempted to choose the shorter stem, because then he can sell a herbicide to kill the tall weeds which would otherwise choke the short-stemmed rice.

And a plant breeder who was also selling fungicides might not be too concerned that his new wheat hybrids were not resistant to wheat rust when he had the appropriate fungicide already on the shelf. Then there is the question of coordinated delivery. Chemical companies are now hard at work developing seed-pelleting techniques so that farmers get their seed pre-coated in chemicals whether they want them or not.

But the marketing of these uniform hybrid seeds does not stop in the West. Most developing countries do not yet have PBR legislation but they are markets for the same seed companies, who naturally wish to sell their products in as many places as possible. According to Dr N.L. Innes of the UK National Vegetable Research Station: 'In the developing tropical world, commercial and state seed companies are fast making inroads.' And he adds that 'now is the time to conserve as many land races and wild varieties as possible.'

In theory the world's genetic resources *are* conserved by an international network of gene banks, where seeds are stored. Central to this network is the international Board of Plant Genetic Resources in Rome. The Board speaks of an 'emerging network' of more than 60 gene banks around the world sharing in this task. In reality however many of these are little more than paper promises and a household-style deep-freeze. None are adequately funded.

The world's genetic Fort Knox is the national seed storage laboratory in the USA. It is trusted with, amongst other things, the world's wheat collection. But it has not had a budget increase for fifteen years; it has only the most rudimentary security precautions and is located midway between a major munitions factory and a nuclear reactor.

There is however a substantial private collection in the hands of the corporations. That may or may not be reassuring. Staff at the major Canadian gene bank report that the private sector has failed to cooperate by divulging information on the genetic material it has in store—two of the culprits are Maple Leaf Mills and Campbell Soup of Canada. The companies can perform a valuable function by incorporating into their own programmes germ plasm that otherwise might have risked extinction. But they do put themselves into a position of political power as the world becomes dependent on them for that crop.

Particularly disturbing for the Third World is that both the important gene banks and the breeding developments which use these genes are in the West. Kenya, for example, is now buying tropical legume seeds developed in Australia based on indigenous Kenyan varieties. There is no record of any payment by Australia for the original material. An identical problem has been reported in Libya where forage seed, exported free to Australia, has been reimported in a slightly altered form at commercial prices—a bizarre situation but one, which makes perfect sense commercially.

The direction that the seed revolution is taking is becoming increasingly clear. While taking what seem reasonable commercial decisions, we could be on the road to disaster. But it is not too late to act. An adequate system of germ plasm conservation *could* save the day. Seeds *could* be freed now from commercial exploitation and patenting. The Third World nations *could* take control of their own valuable plant resources instead of letting them be squandered by the West. There is still, just, the chance to avoid irreparable damage to global food resources.

Session 9

LAND AND FARMING
IN THE
UNITED STATES

Bible Study and Discussion

Leviticus 25

- Read and discuss the passage from the Old Testament Book of Leviticus. This is a long passage, and thought should be given to its reading.
- Discuss the idea of a Sabbath Year and the Year of Jubilee. Can these two concepts be lifted above the sphere of economics? What are the spiritual implications of a year devoted totally to renewal?
- Are the precepts of Leviticus 25 frozen in an historical, agrarian time?

Moving Along

- Do you agree with the statement in the essay "Land and Farming in the United States" (p. 121) that ". . . the future of rural America, seen by many as our most vital institution, is now in question"? Please explain your answer. Be specific.
- After reading Selections A and B (pp. 126–129), what conclusions can you draw about farming in the United States?
- Recall your discussion concerning appropriate technology in the previous session "Technology." Does organic farming have a future? Will the price of petrochemicals affect this issue?

Preparing for the next Session

- The next session is the last. Consider ways in which the group can adequately end their time together.
- Plan a closing liturgy.
- Ask the participants to begin suggesting a follow-up to your deliberations.
- Identify a moderator for the next session.

Ending

- Read aloud:

     Luke 4:16–21
- Pause for silent meditation and reflection.
- Share the prayers written by the participants.
- The moderator and participants say responsively:

     For the Nation

     Moderator:

     Almighty God, giver of all good things:
     We thank you for the natural majesty and beauty of this land.
     They restore us, though we often destroy them.

     Participants: *Heal us.*
     We thank you for the great resources of this nation. They make
     us rich, though we often exploit them.
     Forgive us.

     We thank you for the men and women who have made this coun-
     try strong. They are models for us, though we often fall short of
     them.
     Inspire us.

     We thank you for the torch of liberty which has been lit in this
     land. It has drawn people from every nation, though we have
     often hidden from its light.
     Enlighten us.

     We thank you for the faith we have inherited in all its rich vari-
     ety. It sustains our life, though we have been faithless again and
     again.
     Renew us.

     Help us, O Lord, to finish the good work here begun. Strengthen
     our efforts to blot our ignorance and prejudice, and to abolish
     poverty and crime. And hasten the day when all our people, with
     many voices in one united chorus, will glorify your holy Name.

And at the Very End

Have the group assess the learning they have gained in the session.
- What did you learn?
- Identify any new insights you gained.
- What issues discussed in the session would you like to know more
  about?

Land and Farming in the United States

Despite a history of relatively low food prices in this country, there is a growing sense that those days are gone forever. Food costs are now rising rapidly with an accompanying squeeze on consumers, especially the poor and the elderly. However, if this problem causes us to look more carefully at farming and land use in the United States, it may in the long run prove beneficial. For the sad truth is that few Americans understand the structure or direction of American agriculture.

For decades U.S. farmers have been considered exemplars of prosperity and productivity. Yet they now find themselves facing increasing debts and mounting threats to their land tenure. In the years since the Second World War, the United States has been viewed as the "bread basket" of the world, with its independent family farms producing an abundance of grain for this nation and others. The large surpluses and resulting storage problem in the 1950s and 1960s tended to confirm this impression. However, the last decade has seen dwindling reserves, inflated fuel costs, erratic weather patterns, and shifting trade patterns, all leading to new questions about the structure and direction of U.S. agriculture. For those concerned about hunger and the stewardship of resources, there is a critical need to understand the present situation of U.S. agriculture.

At the core of most people's perceptions of U.S. agriculture is the image of the family farm. While there is much in this image of the individual owner-operator that remains true, it is only part of the picture. Our perceptions are partly shaped by the Jeffersonian ideal that envisoned a nation of yeoman farmers, independent and productive. Yet this world has vanished. In 1950, there were over 5½ million farms in the United States; in 1975, there were less than 3 million. This trend has continued into the 1980s, with concern about this change being more apparent than any ready solutions are. Thus the future of rural America, seen by many as our most vital institution, is now in question.

Former Secretary of Agriculture Earl Butz saw this shift towards fewer and larger farms as a good and necessary one. His advice to farmers can be summed up as "get big or get out." To a large number of people, the old vision of many small operators is hopelessly romantic and unrealistic; yet the current change is being resisted by those who see smaller farms as viable and economical units of production.

For them, such farms are more environmentally sound than larger units and necessary to the preservation of the health of rural communities. Studies done by the Department of Agriculture and by special commissions in California have shown the family farm does provide benefits for rural life and efficient food production. As one small-town banker has said:

> If we could succeed in satisfactorily disposing of the family farm, which seems almost inevitable to many in the light of recent history, then I am almost certain that a vast majority of the some nine million small stores, small banks, professional people, and small communities that these people serve will disappear from the rural scene along with the family farm. (V. E. Rossiter, Sr. President, Bank of Harrington, Nebraska; in "Can the Family Farm Survive?")

Despite their essential contribution to the health of rural communities, family farms continue to disappear. Why? Among the reasons suggested are: (1) the high cost of land and machinery prevents newcomers and young people from purchasing existing farms; (2) energy costs and new equipment investments place a heavy debt burden on farmers; (3) farmers are in a poor situation in the wholesale market, especially when facing the strength of large, vertically integrated businesses (see Dan Morgan, *Merchants of Grain,* for an excellent example); (4) various federal food pricing programs hold down farmers' earnings relative to inflation and costs of production; (5) these same programs provide more funds for larger as opposed to smaller producers.

In a consultation on family farms, the Lutheran Church in American has stated:

> A hallmark of American agriculture has been its increased efficiency. Production capabilities have increased. Research has been conducted and new technologies have been applied. Generally, improved management techniques have been adopted. And yet, a startlingly large percentage of farmer-producers are becoming increasingly helpless in obtaining minimal returns on management, labor, investments, and production costs. Historically, family farms of all kinds have weathered periodic ups and downs of profitability. Many of us believe that neither the present marketplace nor current governmental regulations and support programs are adequate in eliminating continued losses.

As difficult as it is to maintain one's farm in many cases, it can be even harder to find land for starting in agriculture. In recent years, prices for land have climbed dramatically as various purchasers, often speculators, bid against each other for farmland—land valued not just as a productive asset, but as a speculation or hedge against inflation. While farmers may be "rich" in terms of the value of their land, like many homeowners it is wealth they cannot use without selling out. At the same time, access to land is restricted to the few who can afford it. Since the average age of a farmer today is in the late fifties, and only a third of retiring farmers are replaced by new ones, the future of family farms is threatened.

One change already occurring is the purchase of land by absentee landlords who then lease it to tenant farmers. Ag Land Fund I, a proposed investment that was terminated by government and public opposition, exemplifies this trend. The fund would have purchased $50 million worth of prime farmland for growing row crops. Tenant farmers would have worked the land, while shares of $100,000 would have been sold off to investors. Concern about land values, taxes, environmental care, and the spread of such funds prompted the opposition, which discouraged the fund's implementation.

In contrast to an ag-fund, the family farm is a specific system of land ownership that has very different economic and cultural ramifications. It guarantees a spread in the ownership of land. Additionally, such a system increases the opportunities for the individual and/or the community to maintain avenues of access to the land. The issue of farm ownership is critical, yet it remains only part of the story. Even within areas of predominantly family farm systems, farmers face new difficulties.

How can the consumer be suffering from drastic price increases for food while the farmer is being burdened by growing debt? One answer can be found in the very resource that has enabled U.S. farms to grow so significantly in size: farm machinery. As farming technology has become not only bigger but more complex, it has been possible for farmers to plant and harvest greater acreage. Thus the changes brought about through mechanization have increased both the need for, and the cost of, machinery and petroleum products. Inflation in prices has pushed up farmers' debts and threatened their tenure.

Technological advances in agricultural inputs have been generally seen as part of a success story. As a result of the influence of agricultural colleges, government funds, and private initiative, generations of machines and chemicals began spreading across the country. They enabled fewer people to accomplish more. By the 1950s, magazines and popular journals were touting a new vista of utopian farms and a life of ease and affluence for the farmer of the future. It was a picture of opulent production and an endless harvest bounty . . . yet something has gone wrong.

Beneath the simple if frustrating picture of rising prices and diminishing returns is a complex interweaving of issues not easily resolved. U.S. agriculture is facing serious questions about land prices, pesticide use, land ownership, soil erosion, and government price supports. To focus on a particular issue such as soil loss reveals the enormous problems that exist in the present system. The interplay between the farmer's need to make a profit—growing food is not a charitable occupation, just an essential one—and the need to preserve the soil is often out of balance. Thus one sees advice to plant "fence row to fence row." Given the disasters of the Dust Bowl and other less well-remembered "natural" calamities, one wonders how such statements stand up to scrutiny.

Part of the problem is that U.S. agriculture has never come to grips with the limitations of even the most modern agricultural systems. Rather than accept the reality of natural boundaries, farmers have too often sought to use their land as they chose without reference to local ecological conditions. As Donald Worster has written with great clarity in his book, *The Dust Bowl:*

> Three times in the twentieth century the grass lands have been assaulted and pushed back to make room for wheat. Following each expansion, a dust bowl has occurred as soon as the drought cycle has come around again. Nature, it should be clear, has limits; They are neither inflexible nor are they constant, but they do exist. Whenever the dust begins to blow we are being told what those limits are. American agriculture, however, persists in believing that it can ignore ecological truths, that it can live and plow and prosper without restraint. Already we have forgotten the debacle and the discipline of the 1930s. If we believe that we can repeat all the old mistakes of overexpansion and escape the consequences, we are heading, as surely as we were in the roaring twenties, for Dust Bowl IV.

Worster's words are not hyperbole. During the latter half of the 1970s, dust clouds rose over parts of Montana and New Mexico as marginal lands literally blew away. Having been planted with wheat during the bust-boom years of the mid-1970s, they could not withstand erosive forces for long. Even on better land the problem has become severe. Dean Freudenberger, agronomist and church consultant on food and farm issues, has estimated that some areas of the Midwest are losing up to a bushel of soil for each bushel of corn harvested. This is a grim situation. It is also a challenge for those concerned about working with farmers to devise new strategies that could help preserve both the soil and the farmer's livelihood.

The agricultural history of our country began with the family farm, and the time has come to reconsider the family farm. The future of the land is intimately connected with the ownership system that evolves over the next two decades. Incentives for good stewardship of the land must be tied to a pricing system that enables the farmer to survive. While the family farm has an investment in land preservation for the future, this is not enough if debts force unsound practices; thus the marketing side of agriculture necessarily relates to the environmental side. The deeper understanding of the natural cycles, the land's own peculiarities, the interrelationships of people and nature is a process that concerns everyone and that cannot be hurried.

Sensitivity to the farmers' plight is also important. Many farm families resent the naive "back to nature" attitude that bids them to forsake all technical advancements and work minuscule plots of land. They also are uncomfortable with the heavy intrusion of government policy into their lives, both in the area of pricing and in the area of environmental protection, which includes such issues as pest control and soil use. A new concern with the environment and rural roots is necessary, and some government involvement cannot be avoided; nevertheless, farmers wish to be heard, for they too are deeply and intimately involved in the problems discussed. Fred Heinkel, president of the Missiouri Farmers Association, cites some of the major problems in *Can the Family Farm Be Saved?*:

> In the name of efficiency, we have bulldozed out windbreaks to create fields large enough to accommodate today's large equipment. This results in increased wind erosion, and could lead to another dust bowl like that of the 1930s. Use of wide multi-row equipment has destroyed many of the terraces created to reduce water erosion. The severe corn blight epidemic of 1970, which destroyed half of the corn crop in some states, reminded us of

the dangers of relying on only a few strains of hybrid seeds for producing the nation's crops. Elimination of the practice of crop rotation has intensified depletion of the soil, and caused a greater reliance upon pesticides, some of which have since been removed from the market because of their alleged detriment to human health.

At some point a new wisdom is needed to help guide food and farm policy in the United States. As Aldo Leopold once wrote: "We abuse the land because we regard it as a commodity belonging to us. When we see land as a community to which we belong, we may begin to use it with love and respect."

SELECTION A
FARMING TWENTY YEARS FROM NOW: GOT 2 MILLION DOLLARS TO INVEST?
by Jonathan Harsch
Reprinted from *The Christian Science Monitor,* August 21, 1980.

If present trends continue, 1 percent of the farms in the United States will control half of this country's food and fiber production by the year 2000—with the 50,000 largest farms producing almost two-thirds of agriculatural output.

This startling picture emerges from a study just released by the US Department of Agriculture (USDA).

The report notes that the concentration of production in fewer hands will naturally be accompanied by far larger farm units. "About 57 percent of farmland is projected to be operated by farms with 2,000 or more acres in 2000," according to the USDA report. In 1974, the comparable figure was 42 percent.

The fewer, larger farms projected for 20 years from now will be substantial business operations, if the report is correct in predicting that "capital requirements will rise to about $2 million of capital assets per farm for farms with sales of more than $100,000—nearly double what was required in 1978."

However, these figures "are not forecasts," cautions the report, which is entitled "US Farm Numbers, Sizes, and Related Structural Dimensions: Projections to Year 2000."

Instead, in the tradition of Dickens's "A Christmas Carol," the report's projections are intended to provide "a boundary notion of where the present trends are likely to lead in the absence of significant changes in the underlying forces," it says.

The report, in fact, anticipates significant changes—reflecting Secretary of Agriculture Bob Bergland's determination to review the entire structure of US agriculture. This latest report is only one of a wide variety of studies being carried out by USDA researchers in order to provide a basis for a thorough restructuring of government farm programs expected when Congress draws up the 1981 farm bill. Secretary Bergland hopes the measure will be a new departure from, rather than the rubberstamping of, previous programs.

The report notes that past government policy has played a major role in establishing the current "trend toward greater concentration—fewer but larger farms." It concludes that "government may find the projections of use for planning research, for projecting revenues and expenditures, and for examining long-term public policy options to influence the structure of agriculture."

The report rejects some current, well-publicized worries. It sees no trend toward the disappearance of the family farm. The well-managed family farm will survive, it says, although young farmers will find it harder to become established as farms grow dramatically in acreage and capital outlay requirements. It also discounts scare stories that city-based corporations and foreign interests will buy heavily into US farming.

Drawing on a number of studies, the report finds that "the amount of farmland controlled by corporations has never been significant and it is unlikely to become so in the near future. . . . Few nonfarm corporations are likely to be attracted to farming unless the profitability of farming improves greatly."

The report seeks to focus attention instead on the tendency of government programs to favor large farms. It states, "A recent ESCS [Economics, Statistics, and Cooperatives Service of the USDA] study reaffirms what is widely known about the programs—that benefits are closely proportional to production volume: The larger farms, although few in numbers, have the highest production and thus receive a disproportionate share of the program benefits. . . ."

The report leaves it to policymakers to decide whether the US government should continue to encourage ever-larger farms in fewer hands each year—so that the 4 million farms in 1959 that dwindled to 2.9 million in 1974, could drop to 1.8 million by 2000.

Overall, the report puts on the public record the USDA view that Congress has a clear choice: Either it agrees to major farm-policy changes next year, or else it will deliberately be endorsing the continued concentration of farm ownership and production.

SELECTION B
ORGANIC FARMING BLOSSOMS INTO FAVOR AT THE US AGRICULTURE DEPARTMENT
by Jonathan Harsch
Reprinted from *The Christian Science Monitor*, August 13, 1980.

An estimated 1 percent of American farmers—or some 25,000 to 35,000—proudly consider themselves organic farmers.

With some help from an unexpected source—the US Department of Agriculture (USDA)—that percentage could start rising sharply. The change is coming, according to Secretary of Agriculture Bob Bergland, because "energy shortages, food safety, and environmental concerns" are combining to push more and more farmers toward organic farming.

Mr. Bergland himself pushed his department in that direction 18 months ago after finding that one of the neighboring farmers back home in Roseau, Minn., had switched to farming his 1,500 acres organically.

The neighbor, Paul Billberg, was showing profits, fine crops, and healthier cattle six years after deciding to cut out the chemicals that he had always used on his soil, crops, and livestock. Mr. Bergland was impressed and ordered the. USDA's Science and Education Administration to study organic faming—the first time this no-chemicals approach has been given serious consideration by the US government.

The result is a thick USDA report released last month which recommends:

- Research programs both to help organic farmers and to encourage conventional farmers to adopt at least some of the organic farmer's methods for conserving energy and natural resources.
- Programs to evaluate and make best use of organic wastes from both rural and urban sources.
- Development of nonchemical means for controlling weeds, insects, and plant diseases—such as by mechanical cultivation, crop rotation, and natural insect predators.
- Development of new crop varieties geared to organic farming rather than reliant on chemical fertilizers and pesticides.
- Studies of the effects of chemical residues in farm products—to follow up on the warnings issued by Rachel Carson's book, "Silent Spring," in 1962.
- Studies of how yields are increased by combining organic and chemical fertilization methods.
- Research into the economics of organic farming to improve management techniques—to make up for the fact that such help in the past has gone only to conventional farmers.
- Land-grant university courses focusing on organic farming, both to benefit US farmers and to develop models for third-world nations.
- More USDA information dealing specifically with organic farming, both for the farmer and for consumers.
- Establishment of marketing systems for foods certified as organically produced—and thus, in theory at least, able to fetch higher prices.

These and other recommendations come as a surprise because they are from USDA experts who previously showed little interest in or respect for organic farming.

But the report shows that after visiting organic farms in the United States, Europe, and Japan, the USDA researchers were quite favorably impressed by "a production system which avoids or largely excludes the use of synthetically compounded fertilizers, pesticides, growth regulators, and livestock feed additives."

The report churns through a variety of case studies and statistics before reaching a general conclusion that there is little difference between crop yields on organic and conventional farms of comparable quality. The report calls for more detailed research to establish what the differences may be. But it also finds that whatever cost advantages conventional farming may have enjoyed in the past are being wiped out by rapidly mounting energy costs.

The report lists a number of ways in which past government policy has favored conventional over organic agriculture. It notes that parts of the price-support system "appear to run counter to conservation goals, thereby discouraging program participation by conservation-minded farmers in general and organic farmers in particular."

Noting that "public policies can either promote or impede the goals of organic farmers," the report goes on to state that "the future of organic farming as a viable option for food and fiber production will depend on the future goals of US agriculture and on public policy in matters concerning energy conservation, natural resources conservation, and environmental protection."

Dr. Richard Harwood, director of the Organic Gardening and Farming Research Center in Pennsylvania, feels the USDA report is a major—and sorely needed—breakthrough.

"This gives official government recognition for the first time to the value of the organic approach to agriculture," he told the Monitor, "and I think it will give some legitimacy to organic farming and open the way to research in government and in the universities."

Dr. Harwood says that perhaps the most remarkable aspect of organic farming today is that it does produce crop yields comparable to conventional farming—despite having government policies, funding, and research programs all directed at supporting conventional farming.

But will organic farming catch on, or is the farming community too committed to its present methods to change?

Perhaps one clue to the answer comes from the USDA's judgment that "agriculture is a dynamic system, and it operates in a changing environment." A major change is the rise in oil prices, and, the report states, "Organic farming incorporates many of the changes farmers might be expected to make in response to inflated prices of energy."

Another clue comes from Roger Schuller, who raises cattle, sheep, and grain on his 3,400 acres in Claremont, S.D. "We would be tickled to death if we weren't forced into using chemical fertilizers and all that," he told the Monitor. "But if your neighbors do it, competition forces you to do it."

It could be that a new policy approach by the USDA, as indicated in its organic farming report, will help Mr. Schuller and his neighbors shake themselves free from their present dependence on increasingly expensive chemical farming methods.

Session 10

TOWARDS JUST AND SUSTAINABLE AGRICULTURE

Bible Study and Discussion
Deuteronomy 8:7–20
John 2:1–12

- Read and discuss the two Biblical passages.
- Use the pasage from Deuteronomy to summarize the Biblical relationship between God, his chosen people, and the land.
- What message of hope do Christians find in the miracle at Cana?
- Does the account of the Marriage Feast at Cana give any clues to Christ's relationship to nature? To the process of change?

Moving Along
- Discuss the seven major pieces of land reform as identified in the essay (pp. 133–137). As a result of previous sessions, would you add any pieces? Would you question any of those listed?
- "Towards Just and Sustainable Land Use Systems" is a short essay. Can the participants, perhaps in small working groups, write an essay that summarizes what you have learned about land use?
- What does "just, sustainable, and participatory" mean?
- Does Lester Brown's article (Selection A, pp. 137–138) say anything about agricultural systems other than socialistic models? Explain.
- What does Worster (Selection B, p. 139) mean by ". . . man's ability to deal with drought is largely determined by his culture and his social system as they influence farming"?

Ending
- Read aloud:
    Psalm 44
    Genesis 41:25–57

• Pause for silent meditation and reflection.
• Read (or sing):
    Hymn 215

> Lord, who at Cana's wedding feast
>   Didst as a guest appear,
> Thou dearer far than earthly guest,
>   Vouchsafe thy presence here;
> For holy thou indeed dost prove
>   The marriage vow to be,
> Proclaiming it a type of love
>   Between the Church and thee.
>
> The holiest vow that man can make,
>   The golden thread in life,
> The bond that none may dare to break,
>   That bindeth man and wife;
> Which, blest by thee, whate'er betides,
>   No evil shall destroy,
> Through anxious days each care divides,
>   And doubles every joy.
>
> On those who at thine altar kneel,
>   O Lord, thy blessing pour,
> That each may wake the other's zeal
>   To love thee more and more:
> O grant them here in peace to live,
>   In purity and love,
> And, this world leaving, to receive
>   A crown of life above.

ADELAIDE THRUPP, 1853, *and* GODFREY THRING,

• Share prayers prepared by participants or other planned concluding liturgy.
• Read together:

You are God *Te Deum laudamus*

You are God: we praise you;
You are the Lord: we acclaim you;
You are the eternal Father:
All creation worships you.
To you all angels, all the powers of heaven,
Cherubim and Seraphim, sing in endless praise:
    Holy, holy, holy Lord, God of power and might,
    heaven and earth are full of your glory.
The glorious company of apostles praise you.

The noble fellowship of prophets praise you.
The white-robed army of martyrs praise you.
Throughout the world the holy Church acclaims you;
  Father, of majesty unbounded,
  your true and only Son, worthy of all worship,
  and the Holy Spirit, advocate and guide.

You, Christ, are the king of glory,
the eternal Son of the Father.
When you became man to set us free
you did not shun the Virgin's womb.
You overcame the sting of death
and opened the kingdom of heaven to all believers.
You are seated at God's right hand in glory.
We believe that you will come and be our judge.
  Come then, Lord, and help your people,
  bought with the price of your own blood,
  and bring us with your saints
  to glory everlasting.

And at the Very End

Have the group assess the learning they have gained in the session.
- What did you learn?
- Identify any new insights you gained.
- What issues discussed in the session would you like to know more about?
- Plan an evaluation of the whole learning experience.

Towards Just and Sustainable Land Use Systems

How do we envision, let alone develop, a just and sustainable system of land use? A "just" system means that the resources are equitably distributed to the point where no one in any country on earth need go hungry or homeless. This "just" order needs to be balanced by "sustainability" so that it does not result in soil loss or environmental deterioration over time. To put these two visions together is not only possible but an essential challenge for today.

The effort to understand our present situation, marked as it is by widespread hunger and environmental abuse, turns us back to our Biblical roots for direction. If the earth is a gift from God as part of Creation, then it is a common heritage that cannot be "owned" in a way that leads to its destruction. Yet, to say that the earth or a part of it belongs to everyone can also mean that no one is truly responsible for it. Thus individual or local cooperative ownership may well be necessary to identify a particular responsibility for the earth's care.

The need for the sharing of the earth's resources can be seen clearly in many developing countries where a close link exists between poverty and the maldistribution of arable land. This inequitable distribution leads not only to human misery but also to the problems of:

1. mass migration to urban areas in search of employment
2. soil erosion due to poor farmers having to work marginal land
3. depletion of soil fertility through the introduction of nonindigenous export crops—peanuts, coffee, sugar, cocoa—which may be harmful to semiarid or tropical soils prevalent in many developing nations
4. unemployment and environmental damage through the introduction of agricultural inputs from other biogeographical regions that are not suited to local needs.

Bringing about significant change in developing countries will often require drastic alteration in land tenure and land use patterns. There is no way of avoiding the fact that this is an issue fraught with conflict and controversy. It involves nothing less than the coerced removal of land, either through enforced sale or confiscation, from the control of small groups of major land holders. Like it or not, this is one of the central sources of conflict in the world today, from the Philippines to El Salvador to Zimbabwe. How to avoid bloody confrontations and increased human suffering is a challenge for all; yet the present order with its quiet violence is intolerable.

Land "reform," however, is an inadequate term if it refers only to tenure/ownership matters. To ensure a just and sustainable system, several major features are needed, including:

1. security of tenure
2. access to credit
3. profitable producer price levels
4. access to markets
5. conservation policies
6. extension services for small farmers
7. right of political organization for rural groups, farmers, and consumers.

No magic solutions exist—no new Green Revolutions—that can be generally applied to many biogeographical and cultural regions. Agricultural research has not yet been focused on the particular circumstances of tropical, grassland, or semiarid regions. A technological "advance" that brings new benefits to one community may bring disaster to another. Properly planned highways and railroads can open new markets for farmers in one area, while in another area they may bring environmental destruction and disarray.

One specific example of environmentally sound land use is visible in range livestock programs instituted in grasslands of developing countries. Such regions have all too often been used as new farm land or have been grazed by cattle, leading to desertification. An alternative to such an unintentional abuse of land resources is available in the "harvesting" of indigenous animals, such as deer, antelopes, and gazelles that eat a variety of grasses without depleting the land's foundation. In Kenya, such ranches could provide thousands of pounds of meat per year without diminishing the land or the herd. This creative use of a land's natural resources is desperately needed today.

Unfortunately, developing countries have usually been seen as simply depositories for technology from developed countries. All too often international corporations are inefficient in transferring those technologies that are particularly needed for specific land systems. Developing indigenous food systems, training agronomists for local programs, building infrastructures, and designing specific plans for each biogeographical region necessitate a pragmatic approach open to a wide variety of situations. If more just and sustainable land use systems emerge, they will be born from new understandings, not old answers.

As Wendell Berry has written:

> The trouble is that "world hunger" is not a problem that can be solved by a "world solution." Except in a very limited sense, it is not an industrial problem, and industrial attempts to solve it—such as the "Green Revolution" or "Food for Peace"—have often had grotesque and destructive results. "The problem of world hunger" cannot be solved until it is understood and dealt with by local people as a multitude of local problems of ecology, agriculture and culture ("The Gift of Good Land," *Sierra,* November–December 1979)."

In looking at the needs of the United States, Wendell Berry's words have applicability as well. No single, simple solution will work for the farms of Western Oregon, Iowa, New Hampshire, and Southern

Arizona. Nevertheless, some lessons can be learned from the problems that we face today. From these lessons may emerge ways in which the church can help guide future choices about land use and access to land tenure. For ourselves, for our children's children, and for our lives of faith, these are necessary choices.

A sensitivity to the concerns of farmers, consumers, and environmentalists will not be easily developed. Yet the church can provide a meeting place for those who feel powerless in our present system, as indeed representatives of all three of these groups now feel. An understanding of the politics and policy choices relating to land use and food production will help in making this possible. A commitment by churches to support the preservation of the family farm can help nurture trust. Overcoming misunderstandings will not be easy, nor an overnight occurrence. Just as some reformers are naive and uninformed about the scale and complexity of farm management, so are some farmers sanguine and lax about the pressures on their land's fertility. Listening to each other's concerns would be a good place to begin.

A number of steps could be taken to promote a just and sustainable land use and tenure system in the United States. They would include:

1. incentives for soil conservation and land preservation
2. tax laws that strengthen family farms, not outside investors
3. access to land through loan and tenancy programs
4. open lotteries for land irrigated by publicly subsidized water
5. direction of government-funded extension services and research towards the needs of family farms
6. development of commodity pricing policies that benefit the smaller farmers, not subsidize the largest landholders
7. alternative sources for in–puts and markets for farmers, by-passing present oligopolies ("the farmer is the optimist who always buys retail and sells wholesale")

All of these steps will emerge from a new public awareness of the problems faced and the opportunities available in our present situation. A new vision is needed of the common heritage of the land and of the challenge to nurture the land carefully to ensure its bounty and its preservation. Such a vision will require a change from seeing the land as endless or as a mere commodity to be exchanged, eroded, paved, or stripped of its richness. To do this will shake the way we have looked at our world and the way we have come to order our lives. Yet our shared future requires nothing more, and our shared faith demands nothing less.

Two pictures clearly stand out in my mind in thinking about the path to a just and sustainable land use system. One is of a little boy on the streets of Tijuana. He is probably six years old, but his stature is that of a two-year-old. He has known hunger for so long that it is a part of his daily diet. No matter how well-fed he is from today on, he will never be able to reach the full potential that he once had. The land his family once owned grows sustenance for someone else. And even though his view from the little hill overlooks the richness of another land, he will never taste it.

The other vision is of a farmer sitting on a hill overlooking his trees, his vines, and his sheep. He loves the land, and he has known it for many, many years. His income has shrunk compared to the prices he must pay to keep his farm going. The value of his land and hence his taxes have risen as a nearby city paves its way out to meet his fences. He sighs, because he has been devoted to this way of life and has shared generously from his harvests with those in need. He wonders what will come after this present generation.

For those who hunger from lack of justice, for those who weep at the despoiling of the earth, the hope is ever present for a new day, a new land, a new vision of what may yet be. To be with them in the hunger, the tears, and the hope is a possibility to be grasped if we dare to believe that even today the earth will bless the Lord.

SELECTION A
KARL MARX WAS A CITY BOY
by Lester R. Brown
Reprinted from *Science*, Vol. 209, No. 4462, 12 September, 1980.

Although the Soviet invasion of Afghanistan has been widely perceived as a show of strength, it has drawn attention to a major Soviet weakness—a growing dependence on foreign grain. The decision by President Carter to embargo grain imports to the Soviet Union underlined this vulnerability. The harsh reality is that the Soviet Union, once a leading grain exporter, is losing the capacity to feed itself.

Historically, the U.S.S.R. was the breadbasket of Europe. As recently as the late 1930's, net grain exports from the Soviet Union and Eastern Europe averaged 5 million tons a year—exactly the same as those from North America. Since then, the food balance has slowly shifted and the Soviet Union has become a food-deficient country. During the mid-1970's, grain imports by the Soviet Union averaged 9 million tons a year; by the end of the decade, they had climbed to some 20 million tons a year. The Soviets had originally planned to import 34 million tons in 1980—the largest amount in the history of any country.

The Soviet agricultural problem is twofold, with each part compounding the other. They have inherited a relatively poor piece of agricultural real estate, and they have designed an agricultural system that is close to being the worst imaginable. Agriculture in the U.S.S.R. is handicapped by low rainfall and a short growing season. The shortage of well-watered, fertile land is a handicap, but not an insuperable obstacle. It might explain why the Soviet Union is not the leading food exporter, but it is not a sufficient explanation of why it is importing so much grain. Japan, for example, is also poorly endowed with agricultural resources, yet with 3 million hectares of land in grain, it manages to satisfy the needs of its 110 million people for rice, and have some left over for export. The Soviet Union, with 260 million people, has 122 million hectares in grain.

The more serious problem facing the U.S.S.R., and the one it appears least able to cope with, is the inefficiency of its agricultural system. The key link between the efforts of people who work the land and the reward for those efforts is weak. Soviet agricultural collectives and giant state farms do not begin to approach the productivity of the family farm system that dominates Japanese and U.S. agriculture.

A group of young American farmers, who recently returned from living on Soviet collective farms on an exchange program, were amazed to see workers leave their tractors promptly at 5 o'clock, regardless of the circumstances. Planting could be weeks behind schedule or a harvest could be threatened by a coming storm, it made little difference. The mentality was that of factory workers leaving their shifts, not that of farmers. This would never happen in Kansas or Iowa. Farmers in the United States would, if necessary, work around the clock to get their corn or soybeans planted. Everyone—husband, wife, and any children old enough to handle the equipment—would take a turn.

The lack of deep personal ties to the land has also led managers of state and collective farms to exploit the soil in order to meet short-term production quotas and advance their own careers. The widespread loss of topsoil and the associated loss of inherent productivity may help to explain why returns on the heavy investment in agriculture are so disappointing. Thane Gustafson, a Soviet scholar at Harvard, explains that Soviet efforts to expand food production must now reckon with "50 years of neglect that have left a legacy of badly damaged soils."

The combination of a relatively poor agricultural resource endowment and one of the most inefficient agricultural systems yet devised helps explain the failure of Soviet agriculture. It virtually guarantees a gap between food consumption and agricultural output. The factory-style organization of agriculture into state farms and large collectives may sound like a good idea, but it does not work very well. Karl Marx was a city boy, and his origins are evident in the shortcomings of Soviet agriculture.

SELECTION B
JUST AND SUSTAINABLE AGRICULTURE

Droughts will come and go on the earth—that much is certain. We may see many more of them in the future if world climate, as some observers argue, is moving into a new, volatile, unpredictable phase, either warming up or cooling off. There have been 200 year droughts in the past; for all we know there may be one in the near future. In any event, man's ability to deal with drought is largely determined by his culture and his social system as they influence farming. He may adapt himself and his institutions to the foreseeable limits of the environment working cooperatively with other organisms to survive, or he may act as though he were autonomous and invulnerable. The first strategy is sometimes less productive in a short-term, quantitative sense, but it is what the oldest farming cultures of the world have always done and it is by that they have endured; they could teach many lessons to ecologically heedless modernizers in agriculture. American farming, on the other hand, has filled up our granaries again and again—but at a high social and environmental cost. To follow such a culture substantially unreformed into the future would be the most foolhardy risk we have yet taken in this country. To export it lock stock and barrel would be unconscionable. (Worster, *The Dust Bowl,* p. 242)

Bibliography

"Let the Earth Bless the Lord"

Anderson, Bernhard, "The Earth Is the Lord's," *Interpretation,* January 1955.

Austin, Richard, "Toward Environmental Theology," *The Drew Gateway,* Winter 1977.

Baer, Richard, "Land Misuse: A Theological Concern," *Christian Century,* October 12, 1966.

Berry, Wendell, "The Gift of Good Land," *Sierra,* November–December 1979.

Bruggeman, Walter, *The Land,* Fortress, 1977.

Jegen, Mary Evelyn, and Manno, Bruce (eds.), *The Earth Is the Lord's,* Paulist, 1978.

Lutz, Charles (ed.), *Farming the Lord's Land,* Augsburg, 1980.

Moule, C.F.D., *Man and Nature in the New Testament,* Fortress, 1964.

Newell, Phillip, "The Earth Is the Lord's," *Church and Society,* July–August 1979.

Santmire, H. Paul, *Brother Earth,* Nelson, 1970.

"Burden of Empire"

Arias, Mortimer, and Arias, Esther, *Cry of My People,* Friendship Press, 1980.

Beckford, George, *Persistent Poverty,* Oxford University Press, 1972.

Camara, Dom Helder, *Revolution Through Peace,* Harper Coliphon, 1971.

Davidson, Basil, *Let Freedom Come,* Atlantic-Little, Brown and Co., 1978.

Engage/Social Action #56, "Third World Development: A Challenge for Christians," (110 Maryland Ave. NE, Washington, D.C. 20002).

Harrington, Michael, *The Vast Majority,* Simon and Schuster, 1977.

Sheets, Hal, and Morris, Roger, *Disaster in the Desert,* Carnegie Endowment for International Peace, 1974.

Stein, Barbara, and Stein, Stanley, *Colonial Heritage of Latin America,* Oxford University Press, 1970.

"Land Ownership"

Beckford, George, *Persistent Poverty,* Oxford University Press, 1972.

Eckholm, Erik, "Dispossessed of the Earth," Worldwatch Paper, no. 30.

Feder, Ernest, *Rape of the Peasantry,* Anchor Books, 1971.

Fisher, Steve, *A Landless People in a Rural Region: A Reader on Land Ownership and Property Taxation in Appalachia,* Highland Center (Rt. 3, Box 370, New Market, TN 37820), 1979.

George, Susan, *How the Other Half Dies,* Allenheld-Osmun, 1977.

Goldschmidt, Walter, *As You Sow,* Allenheld, Osmun and Co., 1978.

Lappe, Frances Moore, and Collins, Joseph, *Food First,* Ballantine, 1979.

New Internationalist, "Growing Inequality," November 1979.

Taylor, Richard, *Economics and the Gospel,* United Church Press, 1973.

Walinsky, Louis (ed.), *Agrarian Reform as Unfinished Business: Selected Papers of Wolf Ladejinsky,* Oxford University Press, 1977.

Youth Magazine, "Appalachia—This Land Is Home to Me," September 1976.

"Land Marginalization"

Brown, Lester, "The Worldwide Loss of Croplands," Worldwatch Paper, no. 24.

Brown, Lester, and Eckholm, Erik, "Spreading Deserts—The Hand of Man," Worldwatch Paper, no. 13.

"How Much Good Land is Left?" *Ceres,* July–August 1978.

Eckholm, Erik, *Losing Gound,* Norton, 1978.

Franke, Richard, and Chasin, Barbara, *Seeds of Famine,* Allenheld, Osmun and Co., 1980.

National Agricultural Lands Study, "Where Have All the Farmlands Gone?" (722 Jackson Place, NW, Washington, D.C. 20006).

Shepherd, Jack, *Politics of Starvation*, Carnegie Endowment for International Peace, 1975.

Technology

Brown, Michael, *Laying Waste*, Pantheon, 1980.

Chancellor, W.J., and Gross, J.R., "Balancing Energy and Food Production," *Science*, April 16, 1976.

Goulet, Denis, *The Uncertain Promise*, IDOC/North America, 1977.

Hayes, Denis, "Repairs, Reuse, Recycling—First Steps towards a Sustainable Society," Worldwatch Paper, no. 23.

Mooney, Patrick, *Seeds of the Earth*, ICDA (Bedford Chambers, Covent Garden, London W.C. 2), 1979.

Norman, Colin, "Soft Technologies, Hard Choices," Worldwatch Paper, no. 21.

Rhoades, J. Benton, "Not By Tractors," *World Encounters*, September 1978.

Steinhart, John, and Steinhart, Carol, "Energy Use in the U.S. Food System," *Science*, April 1974.

Additional Resources on Women

Hunger Notes: August 1978, "Women and Development"

March 1980, "Agrarian Reform: A Women's Issue at Mid-Decade"

New Internationalist: special issues, July and August 1980

Ceres: "The Right to Work: For Nothing," May–June 1980

Newland, Kathleen, "Women, Men and the Division of Labor," Worldwatch Paper, no. 37.

Additional Resources on Population

New Internationalist: "Population Special," June 1977

"Population: Whose Problem?" September 1979

Scientific America: "Food and Population," September 1974

U.S. Agriculture

Berry, Wendell, *The Unsettling of America*, Avon Books, 1977.

Church of the Brethren, "This Land: Ours for a Season" (110 Maryland Ave., NE, Washington, D.C. 20002).

Engage/Social Action #45, "Can the Family Farm Be Saved?"

Goldschmidt, Walter, *As You Sow*.

Hunger Notes, "Inflation and Food," February 1980.

National Family Farm Coalition, "Agricultural Fact Sheet" (National Family Farm Coalition, 918 F Street, NW, Second Floor, Washington, D.C. 20004).

National Family Farm Coalition, "Who's Squeezing the Consumer?"

The New York Times: "The Peril of Vanishing Farmland," July 1, 1980

"In Plymouth County, Iowa, the Rich Topsoil's Going Fast," July 11, 1980

Ognibene, Peter, "Vanishing Farmlands: Selling Out the Soil," *Saturday Review,* May 1980.

Toole, K. Ross, *The Rape of the Great Plains,* Atlantic-Little, Brown and Co., 1976.

Worster, Donald, *The Dust Bowl,* Oxford University Press, 1979.

Just and Sustainable Agriculture

Dorner, Peter, and Kanel, Don, "The Economic Case for Land Reform: Employment, Income, Distribution and Productivity," Land Tenure Center Reprint, no. 74.

Dubos, Rene, and Ward, Barbara, *Only One Earth,* Norton, 1971.

Hunger Notes, "Agrarian Reform: Who Needs It?" February 1979.

Grigg, D. B., *The Agricultural Systems of the World,* Cambridge University Press, 1974.

McGinnis, Jim, *Bread and Justice,* Paulist, 1979.

Sider, Ron, *Cry Justice: The Bible on Hunger and Poverty,* Paulist, 1980.

Sider, Ron, "Sharing the Wealth: The Church as Biblical Model for Public Policy," *Christian Century,* June 8–15, 1977.

Organizations and Resources

National Hunger Office of the Episcopal Church, 815 Second Avenue, New York, N.Y. 10017

Agenda, (magazine of Agency for International Development), AID Office for Public Affairs, Washington, D.C. 20523

Appalachian People's Service Organization, P.O. Box 1007, Blacksburg, Va. 24060

Bread for the World, 32 Union Square East, New York, N.Y. 10003

Ceres, (magazine of the Food and Agricultural Organization of the UN), UNIPUB, P.O. Box 433, Murray Hill Station, New York, N.Y. 10016

Interreligious Taskforce on U.S. Food Policy, 110 Maryland Ave., NE, Washington, D.C. 20002

Institute for Food and Development Policy, 2588 Mission St., San Francisco, Ca. 94110

Land Tenure Center, University of Wisconsin, Madison, Wis. 53706

National Family Farm Coalition, 918 F Street NW, Second Floor, Washington, D.C. 20004

New Internationalist, (British magazine on development issues), 113 Atlantic Avenue, Brooklyn, N.Y. 11201

Rural America, 1346 Connecticut Ave., NW, Washington, D.C. 20036

Worldwatch Institute, 1776 Massachusetts Ave., NW, Washington, D.C. 20036

U.S. Farmer Organizations

American Farm Bureau

American Agricultural Movement

National Farmers Organization

National Farmers Union